Table of Contents

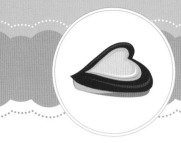

Chunky Oatmeal Raisin Cookies

1 package (about 18 ounces) yellow cake mix
1½ cups old-fashioned oats
½ cup all-purpose flour
2 teaspoons ground cinnamon
½ cup packed brown sugar
2 eggs
1 teaspoon vanilla
1 cup (2 sticks) unsalted butter, melted
1 cup raisins
1 cup walnut pieces, toasted

1. Preheat oven to 375°F. Line cookie sheets with parchment paper.

2. Combine cake mix, oats, flour and cinnamon in medium bowl. Beat brown sugar, eggs and vanilla in large bowl with electric mixer at medium speed until blended. Beat in dry ingredients and butter until combined. Stir in raisins and walnuts.

3. Drop dough by tablespoonfuls 2 inches apart onto prepared cookie sheets. Bake 14 to 16 minutes or until bottoms are golden brown. Cool on cookie sheets 2 minutes. Remove to wire racks; cool completely.

Makes about 4 dozen cookies

Prep Time: 15 minutes
Bake Time: 14 to 16 minutes

Hermits

6 tablespoons (¾ stick) unsalted butter, softened
¼ cup packed dark brown sugar
1 egg
1 package (about 18 ounces) yellow cake mix with pudding in the mix
⅓ cup molasses
1 teaspoon ground cinnamon
¼ teaspoon baking soda
¾ cup raisins
¾ cup chopped pecans
2 tablespoons plus 1½ teaspoons maple syrup
1 tablespoon butter, melted
¼ teaspoon maple flavoring
¾ cup powdered sugar

1. Preheat oven to 375°F. Line cookie sheets with parchment paper.

2. Beat softened butter and brown sugar in large bowl with electric mixer at medium speed until well blended. Beat in egg. Add cake mix, molasses, cinnamon and baking soda; beat just until blended. Stir in raisins and pecans. Drop dough by rounded tablespoonfuls 1½ inches apart onto prepared cookie sheets.

3. Bake 13 to 15 minutes or until set. Cool on cookie sheets 5 minutes. Remove to wire racks; cool completely.

4. Combine maple syrup, melted butter and maple flavoring in medium bowl. Add powdered sugar, ¼ cup at a time, stirring until smooth. Spread glaze over cookies; let stand 30 minutes or until set.   *Makes about 4 dozen cookies*

Apricot Drops

1 package (about 18 ounces) yellow cake mix with pudding in the mix
½ cup all-purpose flour
½ cup vegetable oil
2 eggs
1 cup chopped dried apricots

1. Preheat oven to 350°F. Grease cookie sheets.

2. Beat cake mix, flour, oil and eggs in large bowl with electric mixer at medium speed until well blended. Stir in apricots. Drop dough by rounded tablespoonfuls onto prepared cookie sheets.

3. Bake 8 to 10 minutes or until golden brown. Cool on cookie sheets 1 minute. Remove to wire racks; cool completely. *Makes about 3 dozen cookies*

Spiky Pretzel Balls

2 cups slightly crushed thin pretzel sticks
1 package (about 18 ounces) carrot or spice cake mix
2 eggs
5 tablespoons butter, melted
1 cup chow mein noodles
1 cup mini semisweet chocolate chips
1 cup butterscotch or peanut butter chips

1. Preheat oven to 350°F. Spray cookie sheets lightly with nonstick cooking spray. Place pretzels in shallow bowl.

2. Combine cake mix, eggs and butter in large bowl until well blended. Stir in chow mein noodles, chocolate chips and butterscotch chips.

3. Shape dough into 1-inch balls; roll in pretzels, pressing firmly to adhere. Place 1 inch apart on prepared cookie sheets.

4. Bake 14 minutes or until dough is no longer shiny. Cool on cookie sheets 5 minutes. Remove to wire racks; cool completely.

Makes about 3 dozen cookies

 *Chunkies and Chewies*

Chocolate Chip-Oat Cookies

1 package (about 18 ounces) yellow cake mix
1 teaspoon baking powder
¾ cup vegetable oil
2 eggs
1 teaspoon vanilla
1 cup old-fashioned oats
¾ cup semisweet chocolate chips

1. Preheat oven to 350°F. Lightly grease cookie sheets.

2. Combine cake mix and baking powder in large bowl. Add oil, eggs and vanilla; beat with electric mixer at low speed until well blended. Stir in oats and chocolate chips. Drop dough by rounded tablespoonfuls 2 inches apart onto prepared cookie sheets.

3. Bake 10 minutes or until golden brown. Cool on cookie sheets 5 minutes. Remove to wire racks; cool completely. *Makes 4 dozen cookies*

TIP

Feel free to customize these cookies by replacing the semisweet chocolate chips with milk, white or dark varieties. You could also use chocolate chunks or mini chips depending on whether you want more the chocolate to have a bigger impact or to be present in every bite.

 *Chunkies and Chewies*

Coconut Clouds

  1 package (about 16 ounces) angel food cake mix
  ½ cup water
  1½ cups sweetened flaked coconut
  1¼ cups slivered almonds, divided

1. Preheat oven to 325°F. Line cookie sheets with parchment paper.

2. Beat cake mix and water in large bowl with electric mixer at medium-high speed 3 minutes or until fluffy. Add coconut and 1 cup almonds; beat until combined. Drop dough by tablespoonfuls 2 inches apart onto prepared cookie sheets. Sprinkle tops with remaining ¼ cup almonds.

3. Bake 18 to 20 minutes or until bottoms are golden brown. Cool on cookie sheets 2 minutes. Remove to wire racks; cool completely.

Makes about 4 dozen cookies

Pastel Mint Swirls

  ⅓ cup coarse or granulated sugar
  1 package (about 18 ounces) devil's food cake mix *without* pudding
      in the mix
  3 eggs
  ¼ cup unsweetened cocoa powder
  ¼ cup (½ stick) butter, melted
  1½ cups small pastel mint chips

1. Preheat oven to 375°F. Place sugar in shallow bowl.

2. Combine cake mix, eggs, cocoa and butter in large bowl just until blended. (Dough will be stiff.)

3. Shape dough into 1-inch balls; roll in sugar to coat. Place 2 inches apart on ungreased cookie sheets.

4. Bake 8 to 9 minutes or until tops are cracked. Gently press 3 mint chips into top of each cookie. Cool on cookie sheets 1 minute. Remove to wire racks; cool completely.

Makes about 4 dozen cookies

Cinnamon Cereal Crispies

½ cup sugar

2 teaspoons ground cinnamon, divided

1 package (about 18 ounces) white or yellow cake mix with pudding in the mix

½ cup water

⅓ cup vegetable oil

1 egg

2 cups crisp rice cereal

1 cup cornflakes

1 cup raisins

1 cup chopped nuts (optional)

1. Preheat oven to 350°F. Lightly spray cookie sheets with nonstick cooking spray. Combine sugar and 1 teaspoon cinnamon in small bowl.

2. Beat cake mix, water, oil, egg and remaining 1 teaspoon cinnamon in large bowl with electric mixer at medium speed 1 minute. Gently stir in rice cereal, cornflakes, raisins and nuts, if desired, until well blended. Drop dough by rounded tablespoonfuls 2 inches apart onto prepared cookie sheets. Sprinkle with half of sugar mixture.

3. Bake 15 minutes or until lightly browned. Sprinkle cookies with remaining sugar mixture. Cool on cookie sheets 2 minutes. Remove to wire racks; cool completely.

Makes about 5 dozen cookies

 *Chunkies and Chewies*

Moon Rocks

1 package (about 18 ounces) devil's food or German chocolate cake mix
    with pudding in the mix
3 eggs
½ cup (1 stick) butter, melted
2 cups slightly crushed thin pretzel sticks
1½ cups old-fashioned oats
1 cup swirled chocolate and white chocolate chips or candy-coated
    semisweet chocolate baking pieces

1. Preheat oven to 350°F.

2. Combine cake mix, eggs and butter in large bowl. Stir in pretzels, oats and chocolate chips. (Dough will be stiff.) Drop dough by rounded tablespoonfuls 2 inches apart onto ungreased cookie sheets.

3. Bake 7 to 9 minutes or until set. Cool on cookie sheets 1 minute. Remove to wire racks; cool completely. *Makes about 5 dozen cookies*

Peanut Blossoms

¼ cup sugar
1 package (about 18 ounces) yellow cake mix
1 cup peanut butter
⅓ cup butter, softened
1 egg
50 milk chocolate kiss candies, unwrapped

1. Preheat oven to 350°F. Spray cookie sheets lightly with nonstick cooking spray. Place sugar in small bowl.

2. Beat cake mix, peanut butter, butter and egg in large bowl with electric mixer at medium speed until well blended.

3. Shape dough into 1-inch balls; roll in sugar. Place 2 inches apart on prepared cookie sheets. Press one candy into center of each ball, flattening dough slightly.

4. Bake 10 minutes or until lightly browned. Cool on cookie sheets 2 minutes. Remove to wire racks; cool completely. *Makes about 4 dozen cookies*

Cranberry Gems

⅔ cup dried cranberries or dried cherries
½ cup granulated sugar
3 tablespoons water, divided
1 package (about 18 ounces) white cake mix with pudding in the mix
2 eggs
2 tablespoons vegetable oil
¼ teaspoon almond extract or vanilla
½ cup powdered sugar
1 to 2 teaspoons milk

1. Preheat oven to 350°F. Lightly grease cookie sheets.

2. Combine cranberries, granulated sugar and 1 tablespoon water in small microwavable bowl. Microwave on HIGH 1 minute. Let stand 10 minutes; drain.

3. Beat cake mix, eggs, remaining 2 tablespoons water, oil and almond extract in large bowl with electric mixer at medium speed until smooth. Drop dough by rounded teaspoonfuls 2 inches apart onto prepared cookie sheets. Top cookies with several cranberries.

4. Bake 10 minutes or until edges are lightly browned. Top cookies with additional cranberries. Cool on cookie sheets 2 minutes. Remove to wire racks; cool completely.

5. Whisk powdered sugar and 1 teaspoon milk in small bowl until smooth. Add additional milk, if necessary, to reach drizzling consistency. Drizzle glaze over cookies; let stand until set.   *Makes about 5 dozen cookies*

Garbage Pail Cookies

1 package (about 18 ounces) white cake mix with pudding in the mix
½ cup (1 stick) unsalted butter, softened
2 eggs
1 teaspoon ground cinnamon
1 teaspoon vanilla
1½ cups crushed salted potato chips
½ cup peanut butter chips
½ cup salted peanuts
½ cup mini candy-coated chocolate pieces

1. Preheat oven to 350°F. Lightly grease cookie sheets.

2. Beat cake mix, butter, eggs, cinnamon and vanilla in large bowl with electric mixer at medium speed 2 minutes or until well blended. Stir in potato chips, peanut butter chips, peanuts and chocolate pieces. (Dough will be stiff.) Drop dough by rounded tablespoonfuls 2 inches apart onto prepared cookie sheets.

3. Bake 15 minutes or until golden brown. Cool on cookie sheets 2 minutes. Remove to wire racks; cool completely. *Makes about 3 dozen cookies*

TIP

The best part about these cookies is that you can add whatever you want. Substitute any variety of nuts for the peanuts, any kind of chips for the peanut butter chips, and any kind of chocolate candy for the candy-coated chocolate pieces.

White Chocolate Cranberry Dippers

   1 package (about 18 ounces) spice cake mix
   1 cup old-fashioned oats
  ⅓ cup vegetable oil
   2 eggs
   1 teaspoon vanilla
2½ cups white chocolate chips, divided
   1 cup dried cranberries
   1 cup chopped walnuts or pecans (optional)
   3 tablespoons vegetable shortening

1. Preheat oven to 350°F. Spray cookie sheets lightly with nonstick cooking spray.

2. Combine cake mix, oats, oil, eggs and vanilla in large bowl until well blended. Stir in 1 cup white chocolate chips, cranberries and walnuts, if desired. Drop dough by tablespoonfuls 2 inches apart onto prepared cookie sheets.

3. Bake 10 minutes or until edges are lightly browned. Cool on cookie sheets 5 minutes. Remove to wire racks; cool completely.

4. Place remaining 1½ cups white chocolate chips and shortening in small microwavable bowl. Microwave on HIGH 15 seconds. Stir until mixture is melted and well blended. (Heat additional 10 seconds, if necessary).

5. Spread sheet of waxed paper on work surface. Dip each cookie into chocolate mixture and allow excess to drip into bowl. Place cookies on waxed paper; let stand until set. *Makes about 1½ dozen cookies*

Prep Time: 25 minutes
Bake Time: 10 minutes

 *Coffeehouse Treats*

Orange Chai Spice Sandwich Cookies

1 package (about 18 ounces) orange cake mix
5 tablespoons butter, melted
2 eggs
1 tablespoon pumpkin pie spice
2 teaspoon ground ginger
1 teaspoon orange extract or vanilla
¼ cup cream cheese, softened
¼ cup prepared creamy vanilla frosting
½ cup orange marmalade

1. Preheat oven to 350° F. Spray cookie sheets with nonstick cooking spray.

2. Beat cake mix, butter, eggs, pumpkin pie spice, ginger and orange extract in large bowl with electric mixer at low speed until well blended. Drop dough by rounded teaspoonfuls 2 inches apart onto prepared cookie sheets.

3. Bake 10 to 12 minutes or until tops are puffed and cracked. Cool on cookie sheets 5 minutes. Remove to wire racks; cool completely.

4. Beat cream cheese and frosting in small bowl with electric mixer at medium speed until well blended. Stir in marmalade. Spread rounded teaspoonful of frosting onto flat sides of half of cookies. Top with remaining cookies.

Makes about 2 dozen sandwich cookies

Prep Time: 20 minutes
Bake Time: 10 to 12 minutes

Pistachio Biscotti

1 package (about 18 ounces) devil's food cake mix
1 cup all-purpose flour
½ cup shelled pistachio nuts, coarsely chopped
½ cup (1 stick) butter, melted
2 eggs, lightly beaten
½ cup milk or white chocolate chips

1. Preheat oven to 350°F. Line cookie sheet with parchment paper.

2. Beat cake mix and flour in medium bowl with electric mixer at low speed until blended. Beat in pistachios, butter and eggs at medium speed until combined.

3. Divide dough in half. Shape each half into 9×5-inch log; place 3 inches apart on prepared cookie sheet.

4. Bake 30 to 35 minutes or until toothpick inserted into centers comes out clean. Cool on cookie sheet 15 minutes.

5. Remove logs to cutting board, peeling off parchment paper. Cut each log diagonally into twelve slices with serrated knife. Place slices, cut sides down, on ungreased cookie sheets. Bake 10 minutes. Turn off heat; let stand in oven 30 to 40 minutes or until crisp. Remove to wire rack; cool completely.

6. Place chocolate chips in small resealable food storage bag; seal bag. Microwave on HIGH 1 to 1½ minutes, kneading bag every 30 seconds until chocolate is melted and smooth. Cut tiny corner from bag; drizzle chocolate over biscotti. Let stand until set.

Makes 2 dozen biscotti

 *Coffeehouse Treats*

Cinnamon-Sugar Knots

¼ cup sugar
¾ teaspoon ground cinnamon
1 package (about 18 ounces) spice cake mix
1 package (8 ounces) cream cheese, softened

1. Preheat oven to 350°F. Combine sugar and cinnamon in small bowl.

2. Beat cake mix and cream cheese in large bowl with electric mixer at medium speed until well blended.

3. Shape dough into 1-inch balls; roll each ball into log about 4 inches long. Gently coil dough and pull up ends to form knot. Place 1½ inches apart on ungreased cookie sheets. Sprinkle with sugar mixture.

4. Bake 10 to 12 minutes or until edges are lightly browned. Cool on cookie sheets 2 minutes. Remove to wire racks; serve warm or cool completely.

Makes about 4 dozen cookies

Prep Time: 15 minutes
Bake Time: 10 to 12 minutes

TIP

The lovely shape of these cookies make them ideal for adding a touch of elegance to morning coffee or afternoon tea. Your guests will never guess how simple they were to make.

 *Coffeehouse Treats*

Carrot Cake Cookies

1 package (about 18 ounces) spice cake mix
½ cup all-purpose flour
½ cup vegetable oil
¼ cup water
1 egg, lightly beaten
½ cup shredded carrots (about 2 medium)
½ cup walnuts, coarsely chopped
½ cup raisins
   Prepared cream cheese frosting

1. Preheat oven to 350°F. Line cookie sheets with parchment paper.

2. Combine cake mix, flour, oil, water and egg in large bowl. Stir in carrots, walnuts and raisins until well blended. Drop dough by rounded tablespoonfuls 2 inches apart onto prepared cookie sheets.

3. Bake 12 to 15 minutes or until bottoms are golden brown. Cool on cookie sheets 2 minutes. Remove to wire racks; cool completely.

4. Spread tops of cookies with frosting before serving.

Makes about 3 dozen cookies

Prep Time: 15 minutes
Bake Time: 12 to 15 minutes

Raspberry Devil's Food Cookie Puffs

1 package (about 18 ounces) devil's food cake mix
2 jars (2½ ounces each) puréed prunes
1 egg
3 tablespoons water
3 tablespoons canola oil
2 tablespoons powdered sugar
7 tablespoons raspberry fruit spread

1. Preheat oven to 350°F. Spray cookie sheets with nonstick cooking spray.

2. Beat cake mix, prunes, egg, water and oil in medium bowl with electric mixer at low speed until well blended. Drop dough by tablespoonfuls 2 inches apart onto prepared cookie sheets.

3. Bake 8 minutes or until cookies puff up and indent slightly when touched. Cool on cookie sheets 1 minute. Remove to wire racks; cool completely.

4. Place powdered sugar in fine-mesh sieve. Sprinkle sugar over cookies. Spoon ½ teaspoon fruit spread onto flat sides of half of cookies. Top with remaining cookies.   *Makes about 2 dozen sandwich cookies*

TIP

Baby food puréed prunes work well in this recipe.

 *Coffeehouse Treats*

Peanut Butter Toffee Chewies

  1 package (about 18 ounces) yellow cake mix with pudding in the mix
  1 cup peanut butter
  ¼ cup (½ stick) butter, softened
  ¼ cup water
  1 egg
  1⅓ cup toffee baking bits, divided

1. Preheat oven to 350°F. Line cookie sheets with parchment paper.

2. Beat cake mix, peanut butter, butter, water and egg in large bowl with electric mixer at medium speed until well blended. Stir in 1 cup toffee bits.

3. Drop dough by rounded teaspoonfuls 1½ inches apart onto prepared cookie sheets. Flatten tops of cookies slightly with back of teaspoon. Sprinkle about ¼ teaspoon remaining toffee bits into centers of cookies.

4. Bake 10 to 12 minutes or until edges are lightly browned. Cool on cookie sheets 5 minutes. Remove to wire racks; cool completely.

Makes about 4 dozen cookies

Prep Time: 15 minutes
Bake Time: 10 to 12 minutes

Blondie Biscotti with Almonds

1 cup slivered almonds
1 package (about 18 ounces) white cake mix
⅔ cup all-purpose flour
2 eggs
3 tablespoons melted butter, cooled slightly
1 teaspoon vanilla
3 tablespoons grated lemon peel

1. Preheat oven to 350°F. Line cookie sheet with parchment paper.

2. Cook and stir almonds in medium skillet over medium heat 1 minute or just until fragrant, stirring constantly. (Do not brown.) Cool completely.

3. Beat cake mix, flour, eggs, butter and vanilla in large bowl with electric mixer at low speed until well blended. Stir in almonds and lemon peel. Knead dough 7 to 8 times.

4. Divide dough in half. Shape each half into 12×2-inch log; place 3 inches apart on prepared cookie sheet.

5. Bake 25 minutes or until toothpick inserted into centers comes out clean. Cool on cookie sheet 25 minutes.

6. Remove logs to cutting board, peeling off parchment paper. Cut each log diagonally into ½-inch slices with serrated knife. Place slices, cut sides down, on ungreased cookie sheets. Bake 10 minutes or until bottoms are golden brown. Cool on cookie sheet 2 minutes. Remove to wire racks; cool completely.

Makes about 4 dozen biscotti

 Coffeehouse Treats

Chocolate Pecan Drops

1 package (about 18 ounces) yellow cake mix
1¼ cups pecan pieces, divided
1 cup (6 ounces) semisweet chocolate chips, divided
½ cup (1 stick) butter, melted
2 eggs

1. Preheat oven to 350°F. Line cookie sheets with parchment paper.

2. Combine cake mix, 1 cup pecans, ½ cup chocolate chips, butter and eggs in food processor. Process until pecans are finely chopped and mixture is well blended.

3. Drop dough by rounded teaspoonfuls onto prepared cookie sheets.

4. Bake 10 minutes or until golden brown. Cool on cookie sheets 2 minutes. Remove to wire racks; cool completely.

5. Place remaining ¾ cup chocolate chips in small resealable food storage bag; seal bag. Microwave on HIGH 20 seconds. Gently knead bag until chips are melted and smooth. Cut tiny corner from bag and squeeze chocolate over cookies. Sprinkle with remaining ¼ cup pecans.

Makes about 4 dozen mini cookies

Prep Time: 10 minutes
Bake Time: 10 minutes

 *Coffeehouse Treats*

Angelic Macaroons

1 package (about 16 ounces) angel food cake mix
½ cup cold water
1 teaspoon almond extract
1 package (14 ounces) sweetened flaked coconut, divided
½ cup slivered almonds, coarsely chopped

1. Preheat oven to 325°F. Line cookie sheets with parchment paper.

2. Beat cake mix, water and almond extract in large bowl with electric mixer at medium speed until well blended. Add half of coconut; beat until blended. Add remaining coconut and almonds; beat until well blended. Drop dough by tablespoonfuls 2 inches apart onto prepared cookie sheets.

3. Bake 22 to 25 minutes or until golden brown. Cool on cookie sheets 3 minutes. Remove to wire racks; cool completely.

Makes about 3 dozen cookies

Cappuccino Cookies

1 package (about 18 ounces) devil's food cake mix
¾ cup milk
8 egg whites
1 tablespoon instant coffee granules
1 teaspoon ground cinnamon

1. Preheat oven to 400°F. Lightly spray cookie sheets with nonstick cooking spray.

2. Beat cake mix, milk, egg whites, instant coffee and cinnamon in medium bowl with electric mixer at medium speed until well blended. Drop dough by rounded teaspoonfuls onto prepared cookie sheets.

3. Bake 5 minutes or until centers are set. Cool on cookie sheets 1 minute. Remove to wire racks; cool completely.

Makes about 4 dozen cookies

 *Coffeehouse Treats*

Chocolate Hazelnut Cookies

½ cup chopped pecans
1 package (8 ounces) cream cheese, softened
½ cup (1 stick) butter, softened
1 egg
1 package (about 18 ounces) devil's food cake mix
1 jar (12 ounces) chocolate hazelnut spread
¼ cup powdered sugar

1. Preheat oven 350°F.

2. Place pecans in small resealable food storage bag. Finely crush pecans with meat mallet or rolling pin. Pour into small skillet over medium-high heat; cook 1 minute or until browned, stirring constantly. Remove from heat; cool completely.

3. Beat cream cheese and butter in medium bowl with electric mixer at low speed 30 seconds or until smooth. Add egg; beat at medium speed until well blended. Add cake mix; beat at low speed 2 minutes or until mixture is smooth. Stir in pecans.

4. Shape dough into 1-inch balls; spray palms lightly with nonstick cooking spray, if necessary, to make handling easier. Place 1 inch apart on ungreased cookie sheets.

5. Bake 8 minutes. (Cookies will appear underbaked.) Cool on cookie sheets 5 minutes. Remove to wire racks; cool completely.

6. Spoon 1 teaspoon chocolate hazelnut spread on top of each cookie; sprinkle with powdered sugar.   *Makes about 4 dozen cookies*

Chocolate Cherry Cookies

    1 package (9 ounces) chocolate cake mix
    3 tablespoons milk
    ½ teaspoon almond extract
10 to 12 maraschino cherries, rinsed, drained and cut into halves
    2 tablespoons white chocolate chips
    ½ teaspoon canola oil

1. Preheat oven to 350°F. Spray cookie sheets with nonstick cooking spray.

2. Beat cake mix, milk and almond extract in medium bowl with electric mixer at low speed until crumbly. Beat at medium speed 2 minutes or until smooth dough forms. (Dough will be very sticky.)

3. Coat hands with cooking spray. Shape dough into 1-inch balls. Place 2½ inches apart on prepared cookie sheets; flatten slightly. Place cherry half in center of each cookie.

4. Bake 8 to 9 minutes or until cookies are no longer shiny and tops begin to crack. Cool on cookie sheets 2 minutes. Remove to wire racks; cool completely.

5. Place white chocolate chips and oil in small microwavable bowl. Microwave on HIGH 30 seconds; stir. Repeat as necessary until chips are melted and mixture is smooth. Drizzle white chocolate glaze over cookies; let stand until set.

Makes about 2 dozen cookies

Sunshine Sandwiches

⅓ cup coarse or granulated sugar
¾ cup (1½ sticks) plus 2 tablespoons butter, softened, divided
1 egg
2 tablespoons grated lemon peel
1 package (about 18 ounces) lemon cake mix with pudding in the mix
¼ cup yellow cornmeal
2 cups sifted powdered sugar
2 to 3 tablespoons lemon juice

1. Preheat oven to 375°F. Place coarse sugar in shallow bowl.

2. Beat ¾ cup butter in large bowl with electric mixer at medium speed until fluffy. Add egg and lemon peel; beat 30 seconds. Add cake mix, one third at a time, beating at low speed after each addition until blended. Stir in cornmeal. (Dough will be stiff.)

3. Shape dough into 1-inch balls; roll in coarse sugar. Place 2 inches apart on ungreased cookie sheets.

4. Bake 8 to 9 minutes or until edges are lightly browned. Cool on cookie sheets 1 minute. Remove to wire racks; cool completely.

5. Meanwhile, beat powdered sugar and remaining 2 tablespoons butter in small bowl with electric mixer at low speed until blended. Gradually add enough lemon juice to reach spreading consistency.

6. Spread 1 slightly rounded teaspoon frosting on flat sides of half of cookies. Top with remaining cookies. Store covered at room temperature for up to 24 hours or freeze up to 3 months.   *Makes about 2 dozen sandwich cookies*

Mint Chocolate Cookies

1 package (about 18 ounces) devil's food cake mix
5 tablespoons butter, melted
2 eggs
2 teaspoons peppermint extract, divided
1 cup semisweet chocolate chips
5 to 6 drops green food coloring (optional)
1 container (16 ounces) vanilla frosting
   Green decorating sugar or sprinkles (optional)

1. Preheat oven to 350°F. Spray cookie sheets with nonstick cooking spray.

2. Beat cake mix, butter, eggs and 1 teaspoon peppermint extract in large bowl with electric mixer at medium speed until well blended. Stir in chocolate chips.

3. Drop dough by rounded tablespoonfuls 2 inches apart onto prepared cookie sheets.

4. Bake 12 minutes or until edges are set and centers are no longer shiny. Cool on cookie sheets 5 minutes. Remove to wire racks; cool completely.

5. Stir remaining 1 teaspoon peppermint extract and food coloring, if desired, into frosting. Spread 2 tablespoons frosting onto each cookie; sprinkle with decorating sugar, if desired.   *Makes about 1½ dozen cookies*

Prep Time: 15 minutes
Bake Time: 12 minutes

 *Cookie Jar Favorites*

Toasted Coconut Pinwheels

1 ¼ cups sweetened flaked coconut
1 package (about 18 ounces) white cake mix
1 package (8 ounces) cream cheese, softened
¼ cup all-purpose flour
1 teaspoon coconut extract or vanilla
¾ cup apricot jam

1. Spread coconut in thin layer in medium heavy skillet. Cook and stir over medium heat 2 minutes or until golden brown. Remove from skillet immediately; cool completely.

2. Beat cake mix, cream cheese, flour and coconut extract in large bowl with electric mixer at low speed until well blended. Place dough between two sheets parchment paper and roll into rectangle about 13×10 inches. Spread jam over dough, leaving ½-inch border. Sprinkle with toasted coconut.

3. Roll dough jelly-roll style starting from long side. (Do not roll paper up with dough.) Wrap and freeze 2 hours or refrigerate 4 hours.

4. Preheat oven to 350°F. Spray cookie sheets with nonstick cooking spray.

5. Slice dough into ¼-inch-thick slices; place 1 inch apart on prepared cookie sheets.

6. Bake 12 to 15 minutes or until set. Cool on cookie sheets 3 minutes. Remove to wire racks; cool completely. *Makes about 3 dozen cookies*

Prep Time: 20 minutes
Chill Time: 2 to 4 hours
Bake Time: 12 to 15 minutes

Chocolate Gingersnaps

¾ cup sugar
1 package (about 18 ounces) chocolate cake mix *without* pudding
    in the mix
1 tablespoon ground ginger
2 eggs
⅓ cup vegetable oil

1. Preheat oven to 350°F. Spray cookie sheets with nonstick cooking spray. Place sugar in shallow bowl.

2. Combine cake mix and ginger in large bowl. Add eggs and oil; stir until well blended. Shape tablespoonfuls of dough into 1-inch balls; roll in sugar. Place 2 inches apart on prepared cookie sheets.

3. Bake 10 minutes or until set. Cool on cookie sheets 2 minutes. Remove to wire racks; cool completely. *Makes about 3 dozen cookies*

Lemon Softies

1 package (about 18 ounces) lemon cake mix with pudding in the mix
½ cup oil
2 eggs
¼ cup all-purpose flour
2 teaspoons grated lemon peel

1. Preheat oven to 350°F. Grease cookie sheets.

2. Beat cake mix, oil, eggs, flour and lemon peel in large bowl with electric mixer at low speed until well blended.

3. Drop dough by tablespoonfuls 2 inches apart onto prepared cookie sheets. Bake 10 to 12 minutes or until lightly browned. Cool on cookie sheets 1 minute. Remove to wire racks; cool completely. *Makes about 3 dozen cookies*

Sweet Mysteries

1 package (about 18 ounces) yellow cake mix with pudding in the mix
½ cup (1 stick) butter, softened
1 egg yolk
1 cup ground pecans
36 milk chocolate kiss candies, unwrapped
Powdered sugar

1. Preheat oven to 300°F.

2. Beat half of cake mix and butter in large bowl with electric mixer at high speed until blended. Add egg yolk and remaining cake mix; beat at medium speed just until dough forms. Stir in pecans.

3. Shape rounded tablespoonfuls dough around each candy, making sure candy is completely covered. Place 1 inch apart on ungreased cookie sheets.

4. Bake 20 to 25 minutes or until firm and golden brown. Cool on cookie sheets 10 minutes.

5. Place waxed paper under wire racks. Remove cookies to racks; dust with powdered sugar.

Makes 3 dozen cookies

TIP

These cookies bring a hint of whimsy to snacktime with the delicious milk chocolate surprise that they are hiding. While they are fantastic anytime, try them while they are still slightly warm for an irresistibly gooey treat.

Gingerbread Cookies

1 package (about 18 ounces) spice cake mix
½ cup all-purpose flour
2 teaspoons ground ginger
½ cup (1 stick) butter, melted
⅓ cup molasses
1 egg, lightly beaten
Decorating icing and candies

1. Combine cake mix, flour and ginger in medium bowl. Beat in butter, molasses and egg with electric mixer at medium speed until combined. Shape dough into disc; wrap and refrigerate 4 to 24 hours.

2. Preheat oven to 375°F. Roll out dough on lightly floured surface to ¼-inch thickness. Cut out shapes using 3- to 4-inch cookie cutters. Place 2 inches apart on ungreased cookie sheets.

3. Bake 10 minutes or until edges are lightly browned. Cool on cookie sheets 3 minutes. Remove to wire racks; cool completely.

4. Decorate with icing and candies as desired.   *Makes about 2 dozen cookies*

Prep Time: 10 minutes
Chill Time: 4 to 24 hours
Bake Time: 10 minutes

Citrus Coolers

1½ cups powdered sugar
1 package (about 18 ounces) lemon cake mix
1 cup (4 ounces) pecan pieces
½ cup all-purpose flour
½ cup (1 stick) butter, melted
Grated peel and juice of 1 large orange

1. Preheat oven to 375°F. Line cookie sheets with parchment paper. Place powdered sugar in shallow bowl.

2. Beat cake mix, pecans, flour, butter, orange peel and juice in large bowl with electric mixer at medium speed until well blended. Drop dough by rounded tablespoonfuls 2 inches apart onto prepared cookie sheets.

3. Bake 13 to 15 minutes or until bottoms are golden brown. Cool on cookie sheets 3 minutes; roll in powdered sugar. Remove to wire racks; cool completely.

Makes about 4½ dozen cookies

Prep Time: 10 minutes
Bake Time: 13 to 15 minutes

Black and White Sandwich Cookies

1 package (about 18 ounces) chocolate cake mix with pudding in the mix
1½ cups (3 sticks) butter, softened, divided
2 egg yolks
½ to ¾ cup milk, divided
1 package (about 18 ounces) butter recipe yellow cake mix with pudding in the mix
4 cups powdered sugar
¼ teaspoon salt
2 tablespoons unsweetened cocoa (optional)

1. Preheat oven to 325°F.

2. For chocolate cookies, beat half of chocolate cake mix and ½ cup butter in large bowl with electric mixer at medium speed until well blended. Add 1 egg yolk and remaining chocolate cake mix; beat just until dough forms. Beat in 1 to 2 tablespoons milk if dough is too crumbly.

3. Shape dough by rounded tablespoonfuls into 36 balls. Place 2 inches apart on ungreased cookie sheets; flatten slightly. Bake 20 minutes or until set. Cool on cookie sheets 5 minutes. Remove to wire racks; cool completely.

4. For vanilla cookies, beat half of yellow cake mix and ½ cup butter in separate large bowl until well blended. Add remaining egg yolk and yellow cake mix; beat just until dough forms. Beat in 1 to 2 tablespoons milk if dough is too crumbly.

5. Shape dough by rounded tablespoonfuls into 36 balls. Place 2 inches apart on ungreased cookie sheets; flatten slightly. Bake 20 minutes or until set. Cool on cookie sheets 5 minutes. Remove to wire racks; cool completely.

6. Cut remaining ½ cup butter into small pieces. Beat butter, powdered sugar, salt and 6 tablespoons milk in large bowl with electric mixer until light and fluffy. Add additional 2 tablespoons milk, if necessary, for more spreadable frosting. If desired, divide frosting in half and add cocoa and 1 tablespoon milk to one half to create chocolate frosting. Spread frosting on flat sides of chocolate cookies. Top with vanilla cookies. *Makes 3 dozen sandwich cookies*

 Cookie Jar Favorites

Chinese Almond Cookies

   1 package (about 18 ounces) yellow cake mix
   5 tablespoons butter, melted
   1 egg
1½ teaspoons almond extract
 30 whole almonds
   1 egg yolk
   1 teaspoon water

1. Beat cake mix, butter, egg and almond extract in large bowl with electric mixer at medium speed until well blended. Shape dough into disc; wrap and refrigerate 4 to 24 hours.

2. Preheat oven to 350°F. Spray cookie sheets with nonstick cooking spray.

3. Shape dough into 1-inch balls; place 2 inches apart on prepared cookie sheets. Press 1 almond into center of each ball, flattening slightly.

4. Whisk egg yolk and water in small bowl. Brush tops of cookies with egg yolk mixture.

5. Bake 10 to 12 minutes or until lightly browned. Cool on cookie sheets 5 minutes. Remove to wire racks; cool completely.

Makes about 2 dozen cookies

Prep Time: 15 minutes
Chill Time: 4 to 24 hours
Bake Time: 10 to 12 minutes

Coconut Lime Bars

1 package (about 18 ounces) white cake mix
1 cup toasted coconut, plus additional for garnish
½ cup (1 stick) butter, melted
1 can (14 ounces) sweetened condensed milk
1 package (8 ounces) cream cheese, softened
   Grated peel and juice of 3 limes
3 eggs

1. Preheat oven to 350°F. Line 13×9-inch baking pan with foil, allowing 2-inch overhang around all sides.

2. Combine cake mix, 1 cup coconut and butter in large bowl until crumbly. Press mixture into bottom of prepared baking pan. Bake 12 minutes or until golden brown.

3. Beat sweetened condensed milk, cream cheese, lime peel and juice in another large bowl with electric mixer at medium speed until well blended. Beat in eggs, one at a time, until well blended. Spread mixture evenly over crust.

4. Bake 20 minutes or until center is set and edges are lightly browned. Garnish with additional coconut. Cool completely in pan on wire rack. Remove foil; cut into bars. *Makes about 2 dozen bars*

Espresso Glazed Walnut Bars

Espresso Glaze (recipe follows)
1 package (about 18 ounce) chocolate fudge cake mix with pudding
   in the mix
5 tablespoons butter, melted
2 eggs
1 package (12 ounces) mini semisweet chocolate chips, divided
2 teaspoons espresso powder or instant coffee granules
2 cups chopped walnuts, divided

1. Preheat oven to 350°F. Line 13×9-inch baking pan with foil and spray lightly with nonstick cooking spray. Prepare Espresso Glaze; set aside.

2. Beat cake mix, butter, eggs, half of chocolate chips and 2 teaspoons espresso powder in large bowl with electric mixer at medium speed until well blended. Stir in 1 cup walnuts. Spread batter in prepared baking pan.

3. Bake 25 minutes or until toothpick inserted into center comes out clean. Sprinkle remaining chocolate chips over top. Let stand 5 minutes or until chocolate is softened. Spread chocolate into thin layer. Sprinkle with remaining walnuts.

4. Cool completely in pan on wire rack. Drizzle with Espresso Glaze; let stand until set. Cut into bars. *Makes about 2 dozen bars*

Espresso Glaze: Combine 1 cup powdered sugar, 1 to 2 tablespoons hot water and 2 teaspoons espresso powder or instant coffee granules in small bowl. Stir until espresso powder has dissolved and mixture is smooth. Makes about ½ cup.

Prep Time: 20 minutes
Bake Time: 25 minutes

 *Bar Cookie Bliss*

Raspberry Almond Squares

1 package (about 18 ounces) yellow cake mix
½ cup sliced almonds, coarsely chopped
½ cup (1 stick) butter, melted
1 jar (12 ounces) seedless raspberry jam
1 package (8 ounces) cream cheese, softened
2 tablespoons all-purpose flour
1 egg

1. Preheat oven to 350°F. Line 13×9-inch baking pan with foil, allowing 2-inch overhang around all sides.

2. Beat cake mix, almonds and butter in large bowl with electric mixer at medium speed until crumbly. Reserve 1 cup mixture; press remaining mixture into bottom of prepared baking pan. Bake 10 to 12 minutes or until light golden brown; cool in pan on wire rack.

3. Spread jam evenly over crust. Beat cream cheese, flour and egg in medium bowl at medium speed until combined. Spread over jam; top with reserved crumb mixture.

4. Bake 18 to 20 minutes or until golden brown. Cool completely in pan on wire rack. Remove foil; cut into bars. *Makes about 2 dozen bars*

Prep Time: 10 minutes
Bake Time: 28 to 32 minutes

Nutty S'mores Bars

2¼ cups graham cracker crumbs (14 whole graham crackers, crushed)
1 cup (2 sticks) butter, melted, divided
3 tablespoons sugar
1 package (about 18 ounces) milk chocolate cake mix with pudding
    in the mix
⅓ cup water
2 eggs
1½ cups mini semisweet chocolate chips, divided
4 whole graham crackers, chopped into ½-inch pieces
1 cup mini marshmallows
1 cup roasted salted peanuts

1. Preheat oven to 350°F. Line 13×9-inch baking pan with foil and spray with nonstick cooking spray.

2. Combine graham cracker crumbs, ½ cup butter and sugar in medium bowl. Press mixture into bottom of prepared baking pan. Bake 10 minutes; cool in pan on wire rack.

3. Combine cake mix, remaining ½ cup butter, water and eggs in large bowl with electric mixer at low speed until well blended. Stir in ½ cup chocolate chips. (Batter will be stiff.) Spread evenly over crust. Bake 25 minutes or until toothpick inserted into center comes out clean.

4. Preheat broiler. Sprinkle chopped graham crackers, marshmallows, peanuts and remaining 1 cup chocolate chips over top. Broil 3 minutes or until marshmallows puff and are lightly browned. Cool completely in pan on wire rack. Cut into bars.   *Makes about 2 dozen bars*

Prep Time: 20 minutes
Bake Time: 38 minutes

Cherry Cheesecake Bars

1 can (21 ounces) cherry pie filling or topping
2 tablespoons water
1 tablespoon cornstarch
1 package (about 18 ounces) cherry chip or yellow cake mix with pudding
  in the mix
½ cup (1 stick) butter, melted
1 egg
1 container (about 24 ounces) refrigerated ready-to-eat cheesecake filling

1. Place cherry pie filling in medium saucepan. Stir water and cornstarch together in small bowl until cornstarch is dissolved. Stir cornstarch mixture into pie filling. Cook and stir over medium heat until mixture comes to a boil. Boil 2 minutes, stirring constantly. Remove from heat; cool completely.

2. Preheat oven to 350°F. Spray 13×9-inch baking pan with nonstick cooking spray.

3. Combine cake mix, butter and egg in medium bowl until well blended. (Mixture will be crumbly.) Press mixture into bottom of prepared baking pan. Bake 15 minutes. Cool completely in pan on wire rack.

4. Spread cheesecake filling evenly over crust. Spread cherry topping over cheesecake filling. Cover and refrigerate 4 to 24 hours before serving. Cut into bars.   *Makes about 2 dozen bars*

Prep Time: 25 minutes
Chill Time: 4 to 24 hours
Bake Time: 15 minutes

 Bar Cookie Bliss

Black Forest Bars

1 package (about 18 ounces) dark chocolate cake mix
½ cup (1 stick) butter, melted
1 egg
½ teaspoon almond extract
1¼ cups sliced almonds, divided
1 jar (about 16 ounces) maraschino cherries, well drained
½ cup semisweet chocolate chips

1. Preheat oven to 350°F. Line 13×9-inch baking pan with foil, allowing 2-inch overhang around all sides.

2. Beat cake mix, butter, egg and almond extract in large bowl with electric mixer at medium speed until well blended. Stir in ¾ cup almonds.

3. Press dough into bottom of prepared baking pan. Top evenly with cherries. Bake 20 to 25 minutes or until toothpick inserted into center comes out clean. Cool completely in pan on wire rack.

4. Place chocolate chips in small resealable food storage bag; seal bag. Microwave on HIGH 1 to 1½ minutes, kneading bag every 30 seconds until melted and smooth. Cut tiny corner from bag; drizzle chocolate over top. Sprinkle with remaining ½ cup almonds; let stand until set. Remove foil; cut into bars. *Makes about 2 dozen bars*

Prep Time: 10 minutes
Bake Time: 20 to 25 minutes

Cobbled Fruit Bars

1½ cups apple juice
  1 cup chopped dried apricots
  1 cup raisins
  1 package (6 ounces) dried cherries
  1 teaspoon cornstarch
  1 teaspoon ground cinnamon
  1 package (about 18 ounces) yellow cake mix
  2 cups old-fashioned oats
  ¾ cup (1½ sticks) butter, melted
  1 egg

1. Combine apple juice, apricots, raisins, cherries, cornstarch and cinnamon in medium saucepan, stirring until cornstarch is dissolved. Bring to a boil; cook and stir 5 minutes. Cool to room temperature.

2. Preheat oven to 350°F. Line 15×10-inch jelly-roll pan with foil and spray with nonstick cooking spray.

3. Combine cake mix and oats in large bowl; stir in butter. Add egg; stir until well blended. Press three fourths of dough into bottom of prepared baking pan. Spread fruit mixture evenly over top. Sprinkle remaining dough over fruit.

4. Bake 25 to 30 minutes or until lightly browned. Cool completely in pan on wire rack. Remove foil; cut into bars.   *Makes about 3 dozen bars*

Prep Time: 30 minutes
Bake Time: 25 to 30 minutes

PB&J Cookie Bars

1 package (about 18 ounces) yellow cake mix with pudding in the mix
1 cup peanut butter
½ cup vegetable oil
2 eggs
1 cup strawberry jam
1 cup peanut butter chips

1. Preheat oven to 350°F. Line 15×10-inch jelly-roll pan with foil and spray with nonstick cooking spray.

2. Beat cake mix, peanut butter, oil and eggs in large bowl with electric mixer at medium speed until well blended. With damp hands, press mixture evenly into bottom of prepared baking pan. Bake 20 minutes; cool in pan on wire rack.

3. Place jam in small microwavable bowl. Microwave on HIGH 20 seconds to soften. Spread jam evenly over cookie base. Sprinkle peanut butter chips over top.

4. Bake 10 minutes or until edges are browned. Cool completely in pan on wire rack. Remove foil; cut into bars. *Makes about 3 dozen bars*

Prep Time: 20 minutes
Bake Time: 30 minutes

Chocolate Peanut Butter Candy Bars

1 package (about 18 ounces) devil's food or dark chocolate cake mix
    without pudding in the mix
1 can (5 ounces) evaporated milk
⅓ cup butter, melted
½ cup dry-roasted peanuts
4 packages (1½ ounces each) chocolate peanut butter cups, coarsely
    chopped

1. Preheat oven to 350°F. Lightly grease 13×9-inch baking pan.

2. Beat cake mix, evaporated milk and butter in large bowl with electric mixer at medium speed until well blended. (Dough will be stiff.) Press two thirds of dough into bottom of prepared baking pan. Sprinkle with peanuts.

3. Bake 10 minutes; sprinkle with chopped candy. Drop remaining dough by large tablespoonfuls over top.

4. Bake 15 to 20 minutes or until center is firm to the touch. Cool completely in pan on wire rack. Cut into bars.   *Makes about 2 dozen bars*

Prep Time: 10 minutes
Bake Time: 25 to 30 minutes

Chocolate Peanut Butter Candy Bars

 Bar Cookie Bliss

Triple Chocolate Cream Cheese Bars

1 package (about 18 ounces) chocolate cake mix
⅓ cup vegetable oil
3 eggs
2 packages (8 ounces each) cream cheese, softened
⅓ cup sugar
1 cup sour cream
1 cup (6 ounces) semisweet chocolate chips, melted and cooled slightly
1 cup white chocolate chips

1. Preheat oven to 350°F. Grease 13×9-inch glass baking dish.

2. Combine cake mix, oil and 1 egg in medium bowl; mix well. Press mixture into bottom of prepared baking dish. Bake 10 minutes or until set; cool in dish on wire rack.

3. Beat cream cheese in large bowl with electric mixer at high speed until light and fluffy. Add remaining 2 eggs and sugar; beat until well blended. Beat in sour cream and melted chocolate until blended. Pour over crust; sprinkle with white chocolate chips.

4. Bake 50 minutes or until set. Cool completely in dish on wire rack. Refrigerate 4 hours. Cut into bars. *Makes about 1½ dozen bars*

Pecan Coconut Layer Bars

1 package (about 18 ounces) yellow cake mix
5 tablespoons butter, melted
3 eggs
¾ cup corn syrup
¼ cup packed brown sugar
1 teaspoon vanilla
1 cup chopped pecans
¾ cup sweetened flaked coconut

1. Preheat oven to 350°F. Line 13×9-inch baking pan with foil and spray with nonstick cooking spray.

2. Combine cake mix, butter and 1 egg in large bowl until well blended. (Dough will be stiff.) Press dough into bottom of prepared baking pan. Bake 15 minutes; cool in pan on wire rack.

3. Combine corn syrup, brown sugar, remaining 2 eggs and vanilla in another large bowl until well blended. Stir in pecans and coconut. Spread mixture evenly over crust.

4. Bake 25 minutes or until top is bubbling and edges are lightly browned. Cool completely in pan on wire rack. Remove foil; cut into bars.

Makes about 2 dozen bars

Prep Time: 15 minutes
Bake Time: 40 minutes

Cinnamon Apple Pie Bars

1 package (about 18 ounces) spice cake mix with pudding in the mix
2 cups old-fashioned oats
½ teaspoon ground cinnamon
¾ cup (1½ sticks) butter, cut into pieces
1 egg
1 can (21 ounces) apple pie filling and topping

1. Preheat oven to 350°F. Spray 13×9-inch baking pan with nonstick cooking spray.

2. Combine cake mix, oats and cinnamon in large bowl. Cut in butter using pastry blender or two knives until mixture resembles coarse crumbs. Stir in egg until blended.

3. Press three fourths of oat mixture into bottom of prepared baking pan. Spread apple pie filling evenly over top. Crumble remaining oat mixture over filling.

4. Bake 25 to 30 minutes or until lightly browned. Cool completely in pan on wire rack. Cut into bars. *Makes about 2 dozen bars*

Prep Time: 15 minutes
Bake Time: 25 to 30 minutes

Lemon Cheese Bars

1 package (about 18 ounces) white or yellow cake mix with pudding
    in the mix
2 eggs
⅓ cup vegetable oil
1 package (8 ounces) cream cheese, softened
⅓ cup sugar
1 teaspoon lemon juice

1. Preheat oven to 350°F.

2. Combine cake mix, 1 egg and oil in large bowl; stir until crumbly. Reserve
1 cup crumb mixture. Press remaining crumb mixture into bottom of ungreased
13×9-inch baking pan.

3. Bake 15 minutes or until golden brown. Cool in pan on wire rack 15 minutes.

4. Beat remaining egg, cream cheese, sugar and lemon juice in medium bowl
with electric mixer at medium speed until smooth and well blended. Spread over
crust. Sprinkle with reserved crumb mixture.

5. Bake 15 minutes or just until set. Cool completely in pan on wire rack. Cut
into bars. *Makes about 2 dozen bars*

 Bar Cookie Bliss

Chocolate and Oat Toffee Bars

¾ cup (1½ sticks) plus 2 tablespoons butter, softened, divided
1 package (about 18 ounces) yellow cake mix with pudding in the mix
2 cups quick oats
¼ cup packed brown sugar
1 egg
½ teaspoon vanilla
1 cup toffee baking bits
½ cup chopped pecans
⅓ cup semisweet chocolate chips

1. Preheat oven to 350°F. Grease 13×9-inch baking pan.

2. Beat ¾ cup butter in large bowl with electric mixer at medium speed until creamy. Add cake mix, oats, brown sugar, egg and vanilla; beat until well blended. Stir in toffee bits and pecans. Press dough into bottom of prepared baking pan.

3. Bake 30 to 35 minutes or until golden brown. Cool completely in pan on wire rack.

4. Melt remaining 2 tablespoons butter and chocolate chips in small saucepan over low heat. Drizzle over top. Let stand 1 hour or until set. Cut into bars.

Makes about 2 dozen bars

Buried Cherry Bars

1 jar (10 ounces) maraschino cherries
1 package (about 18 ounces) devil's food cake mix *without* pudding
    in the mix
1 cup (2 sticks) butter, melted
1 egg
½ teaspoon almond extract
1½ cups semisweet chocolate chips
¾ cup sweetened condensed milk
½ cup chopped pecans

1. Preheat oven to 350°F. Lightly grease 13×9-inch baking pan. Drain cherries, reserving 2 tablespoons juice. Cut cherries into quarters.

2. Combine cake mix, butter, egg and almond extract in large bowl until blended. (Batter will be very thick.) Stir in cherries. Spread batter in prepared baking pan.

3. Combine chocolate chips and sweetened condensed milk in small saucepan. Cook over low heat until chocolate is melted, stirring constantly. Stir in reserved cherry juice. Spread chocolate mixture evenly in pan; sprinkle with pecans.

4. Bake 35 minutes or until center is set. Cool completely in pan on wire rack. Cut into bars.

Makes about 2 dozen bars

 Bar Cookie Bliss

Apricot Crumb Squares

1 package (about 18 ounces) yellow cake mix
1 teaspoon ground cinnamon
½ teaspoon ground nutmeg
¼ cup (½ stick) plus 2 tablespoons butter, cut into pieces
¾ cup old-fashioned oats
1 egg
2 egg whites
1 tablespoon water
1 jar (10 ounces) apricot fruit spread
2 tablespoons packed light brown sugar

1. Preheat oven to 350°F.

2. Combine cake mix, cinnamon and nutmeg in medium bowl. Cut in butter with pastry blender or two knives until mixture resembles coarse crumbs. Stir in oats. Reserve 1 cup crumb mixture. Add egg, egg whites and water to remaining crumb mixture; stir until well blended.

3. Spread evenly in ungreased 13×9-inch baking pan; top with fruit spread. Sprinkle reserved crumb mixture over fruit spread; sprinkle with brown sugar.

4. Bake 35 to 40 minutes or until golden brown. Cool completely in pan on wire rack. Cut into bars.   *Makes about 2 dozen bars*

Table of Contents

Key Lime Angel Food Torte

    1 package (about 16 ounces) angel food cake mix, plus ingredients
        to prepare mix
    1 can (14 ounces) sweetened condensed milk
    ⅔ cup bottled key lime juice
    1 container (8 ounces) whipped topping
    ⅓ cup shredded coconut
        Peel of 1 lime

1. Preheat oven to 350°F. Prepare and bake cake mix in ungreased 10-inch tube pan according to package directions. Invert pan onto wire rack; cool completely in pan.

2. For filling, whisk sweetened condensed milk and lime juice in medium bowl until smooth. Fold in whipped topping. Cover and refrigerate until ready to use.

3. Loosen side of cake with knife; remove cake from pan. With bottom side up, cut cake horizontally into four layers.

4. Place widest cake layer, cut side up, on serving platter; spread with one fourth of filling. Repeat layers twice. Top with remaining cake layer. Spread with remaining filling, allowing some to run down side of cake. Sprinkle with coconut and lime peel; refrigerate 1 hour or until set.   *Makes 12 servings*

TIP

When making angel food cake, it's important not to grease the pan so that the batter can grip the side and rise as high as possible. Using a tube pan with a removable bottom will make releasing the cake much easier.

Chocolate Lovers' Cake

1 package (about 18 ounces) chocolate cake mix, plus ingredients
    to prepare mix
3 tablespoons seedless raspberry preserves, warmed
  Chocolate Ganache (recipe follows)
  Chocolate Shapes (recipe follows)
⅔ cup sweetened condensed milk
1 cup (6 ounces) semisweet chocolate chips
1 tablespoon butter

1. Prepare and bake cake mix in two 8- or 9-inch pans according to package directions. Cool in pans 10 minutes. Remove to wire racks; poke holes into tops of layers with toothpick. Brush with melted preserves. Cool completely.

2. Prepare Chocolate Ganache and Chocolate Shapes. For filling, combine sweetened condensed milk, chocolate chips and butter in small heavy saucepan. Cook over low heat until chips are melted and mixture is smooth. Cool slightly.

3. Place one cake layer on serving plate; spread filling evenly over cake. Top with remaining cake layer. Frost cake with Chocolate Ganache; top with Chocolate Shapes. *Makes 12 servings*

Chocolate Ganache: Combine ¾ cup whipping cream, 1 tablespoon butter and 1 tablespoon sugar in small saucepan; bring to a boil over medium-high heat, stirring until sugar is dissolved. Place 1½ cups semisweet chocolate chips in medium bowl. Pour cream mixture over chocolate; let stand 5 minutes. Stir until smooth; let stand 15 minutes or until ganache reaches desired consistency. (Ganache will thicken as it cools.) Makes about 1½ cups.

Chocolate Shapes: Place sheet of waxed paper on inverted baking sheet. Place ⅓ cup semisweet chocolate chips in resealable food storage bag; microwave on HIGH 1 minute. Knead bag. Microwave additional 10 to 20 seconds until chocolate is melted and smooth. Cut off tiny corner of bag. Pipe chocolate in desired shapes on waxed paper. Let stand until set. (Do not refrigerate.) Gently peel shapes off waxed paper.

Banana Supreme Cake

       1 package (about 18 ounces) yellow cake mix
1¼ cups water
       3 eggs
⅓ cup vegetable oil
       1 teaspoon vanilla
          Vanilla Cream Cheese Icing (recipe follows)
       3 ripe bananas, sliced
       1 cup lemon-lime soda
       3 cups milk
       1 package (4-serving size) vanilla instant pudding and pie filling mix
½ cup chopped walnuts (optional)

1. Preheat oven to 350°F. Grease and flour two 9-inch round cake pans.

2. Beat cake mix, water, eggs, oil and vanilla in large bowl with electric mixer at medium speed until smooth. Pour batter into prepared pans. Bake 25 minutes or until toothpick inserted into centers comes out clean. Cool completely in pans on wire racks.

3. Prepare Vanilla Cream Cheese Icing. Soak sliced bananas in soda. Combine milk and pudding mix in medium bowl. Beat until pudding begins to thicken.

4. Place one cake layer on serving plate. Top with half of pudding mixture. Arrange sliced bananas over top. Spoon remaining pudding over bananas. Top with remaining cake layer. Frost cake with Vanilla Cream Cheese Icing. Garnish with walnuts. Keep refrigerated.   *Makes 10 to 12 servings*

Vanilla Cream Cheese Icing

       2 containers (8 ounces each) whipped topping
       1 package (8 ounces) cream cheese, softened
       3 tablespoons hot water
       2 tablespoons powdered sugar
       1 teaspoon vanilla

Beat all ingredients in large bowl with electric mixer at medium speed until creamy and smooth.   *Makes about 4 cups*

Black Forest Angel Food Cake

  1 package (about 16 ounces) angel food cake mix
  ½ cup unsweetened cocoa powder
1½ cups water
  1 can (12 ounces) cherry pie filling
  2 tablespoons cherry liqueur (optional)
  1 cup whipping cream
  2 tablespoons powdered sugar

1. Preheat oven to 350°F.

2. Pour cake mix into large bowl; sift cocoa over top. Add water; whisk 2 minutes or until well blended. Pour batter into ungreased 10-inch tube pan. Bake and cool according to package directions.

3. Place cherry pie filling in medium microwavable bowl; microwave on HIGH 1 minute or until heated through. Stir in liqueur, if desired.

4. Beat cream and sugar in medium bowl with electric mixer at medium-high speed until stiff peaks form. Cut cake horizontally into three layers. Place widest layer, cut side up, on serving plate. Top with half of whipped cream and cherries. Repeat layers. Top with remaining cake layer.

Makes 12 to 16 servings

Layered Chocolate Torte

1 package (about 16 ounces) pound cake mix, plus ingredients
  to prepare mix
6 ounces bittersweet chocolate, broken into pieces
1 container (8 ounces) whipped topping
¼ cup plus 2 tablespoons sour cream
  Chocolate curls (optional)

1. Preheat oven to 400°F. Line 15×10-inch jelly-roll pan with parchment paper. Prepare cake mix according to package directions. Spread batter evenly in prepared pan.

2. Bake 12 to 14 minutes or until toothpick inserted into center comes out clean. Cool in pan 10 minutes. Remove from pan (lift cake and parchment up together to easily slide cake out of pan); cool completely on wire rack.

3. Place chocolate in medium microwavable bowl; microwave on HIGH 1 minute or until melted, stirring after 30 seconds. Cool slightly; fold in whipped topping and sour cream until well blended.

4. Place cake on cutting board; cut crosswise into four equal pieces. Place one cake layer on serving plate; spread with chocolate mixture. Repeat layers twice. Top with remaining cake layer. Frost cake with remaining chocolate mixture. Refrigerate 1 hour before serving. Garnish with chocolate curls.

Makes about 12 servings

Dark Chocolate Coconut Cake

1 package (about 18 ounces) devil's food cake mix, plus ingredients
    to prepare mix
1 cup strong coffee
½ cup evaporated milk
4 tablespoons butter, divided
3 cups mini marshmallows*
1 package (14 ounces) shredded coconut
1 cup whipping cream
2 cups (12 ounces) semisweet chocolate chips**

*Or substitute 24 large marshmallows.

**For more intense chocolate flavor, use bittersweet or dark chocolate chips.

1. Preheat oven to 350°F. Coat two 8-inch cake pans with nonstick cooking spray. Prepare cake mix according to package directions, substituting coffee for water. Pour batter evenly into prepared pans.

2. Bake 23 to 25 minutes or until toothpick inserted into centers comes out clean. Cool completely in pans on wire racks.

3. For filling, bring evaporated milk and 2 tablespoons butter to a boil in medium saucepan over medium heat. Add marshmallows; stir until smooth. Stir in coconut. Cool completely.

4. For topping, heat cream and remaining 2 tablespoons butter in medium saucepan over medium-low heat. (Do not boil.) Remove from heat; add chocolate chips. Let stand 1 minute; stir until smooth.

5. Cut each cake layer in half horizontally. Place one cake layer on serving plate; spread with one third of filling almost to edge. Repeat layers twice. Top with remaining cake layer. Frost cake with topping. Refrigerate until topping is set. Store leftovers in refrigerator. *Makes 12 to 16 servings*

Delicious Strawberry Torte

    4 eggs, separated
    1 package (about 18 ounces) yellow cake mix
1 ⅓ cups milk
    1 package (4-serving size) vanilla instant pudding and pie filling mix
    ¼ cup vegetable oil
    1 teaspoon vanilla
      Icing (recipe follows)
    1 quart strawberries, stemmed and halved
      Whole strawberries (optional)

1. Preheat oven to 375°F. Grease and flour two 9-inch round cake pans.

2. Beat egg whites in medium bowl with electric mixer at high speed until soft peaks form. Beat cake mix, milk, pudding mix, egg yolks, oil and vanilla in large bowl at medium speed until well blended. Fold in egg whites. Pour batter into prepared pans.

3. Bake 28 to 32 minutes or until toothpick inserted into centers comes out clean. Cool in pans 15 minutes. Remove to wire racks; cool completely. Meanwhile, prepare Icing.

4. Cut each cake layer in half horizontally. Place one cake layer on serving plate. Spread with one fourth of Icing; top with one third of strawberry halves. Repeat layers twice. Top with remaining cake layer. Spread with remaining Icing. Garnish with whole strawberries.   *Makes 10 to 12 servings*

Icing

    1 package (8 ounces) cream cheese, softened
    1 container (8 ounces) whipped topping
    1 cup granulated sugar
    1 cup powdered sugar
    ¼ cup butter, softened
    1 teaspoon vanilla

Beat all ingredients in medium bowl with electric mixer at medium speed until smooth. Refrigerate until ready to use.   *Makes about 3 cups*

Chocolatey Bananas Foster Cake

1 package (about 18 ounces) devil's food cake mix
1 cup mashed bananas*
3 eggs
⅓ cup vegetable oil
¼ cup water
¼ cup packed brown sugar
2 tablespoons butter
¾ cup finely chopped firm ripe bananas
½ teaspoon rum extract
¼ teaspoon ground cinnamon
2 cups whipping cream
¼ cup powdered sugar

*Overripe bananas provide the most intense banana flavor.

1. Preheat oven to 350°F. Coat two 8-inch round cake pans with nonstick cooking spray.

2. Beat cake mix, mashed bananas, eggs, oil and water in large bowl with electric mixer at low speed 30 seconds. Beat at medium speed 2 minutes. Pour batter into prepared pans.

3. Bake 23 to 25 minutes or until toothpick inserted into centers comes out clean. Cool in pans 15 minutes. Remove to wire racks; cool completely.

4. Combine brown sugar and butter in small saucepan over medium-low heat; cook and stir until smooth. Add chopped bananas, rum extract and cinnamon; cook and stir until mixture thickens slightly. Cool completely.

5. Beat cream and powdered sugar in medium bowl with electric mixer at high speed until stiff peaks form.

6. Place one cake layer on serving plate. Spread with half of whipped cream; spoon banana mixture evenly over cream. Top with remaining cake layer. Frost cake with remaining whipped cream. Store leftovers in refrigerator.

Makes 12 servings

 Luscious Layers

Celebration Pumpkin Cake

1 package (about 18 ounces) spice cake mix
1 can (15 ounces) solid-pack pumpkin
3 eggs
¼ cup (½ stick) butter, softened
1½ containers (16 ounces each) cream cheese frosting
⅓ cup caramel ice cream topping
Pecan halves (optional)

1. Preheat oven to 350°F. Grease and flour three 9-inch round cake pans.

2. Beat cake mix, pumpkin, eggs and butter in large bowl with electric mixer at medium speed until blended. Pour batter into prepared pans.

3. Bake 20 minutes or until toothpick inserted into centers comes out clean. Cool in pans 15 minutes. Remove to wire racks; cool completely.

4. Place one cake layer on serving plate; spread with one fourth of frosting. Repeat layers. Top with remaining cake layer. Frost cake with remaining frosting. Spread caramel topping over top of cake, allowing some to drip down side. Garnish with pecans.

Makes 12 servings

Candy Bar Cake

1 package (about 18 ounces) devil's food cake mix *without* pudding
    in the mix
1 cup sour cream
4 eggs
⅓ cup vegetable oil
¼ cup water
2 containers (16 ounces each) white frosting
1 bar (about 2 ounces) chocolate-covered crispy peanut butter
    candy, chopped
1 bar (about 2 ounces) chocolate-covered peanut, caramel and
    nougat candy, chopped
1 bar (about 1½ ounces) chocolate-covered toffee candy, chopped
4 bars (about 1½ ounces each) milk chocolate

1. Preheat oven to 350°F. Grease and flour two 9-inch round cake pans.

2. Beat cake mix, sour cream, eggs, oil and water in large bowl with electric mixer at low speed until blended. Beat at medium speed 2 minutes or until smooth. Pour batter into prepared pans.

3. Bake 30 to 35 minutes or until toothpick inserted into centers comes out clean. Cool in pans 10 minutes. Remove to wire racks; cool completely.

4. Cut each cake layer in half horizontally. Place one cake layer on serving plate. Spread generously with frosting. Sprinkle with one chopped candy bar. Repeat layers twice. Top with remaining cake layer. Spread remaining frosting on top of cake.

5. Break milk chocolate bars into pieces along score lines. Arrange chocolate pieces around top edge of cake. *Makes 12 servings*

Rum and Spumone Layered Torte

1 package (about 18 ounces) butter recipe yellow cake mix
3 eggs
½ cup (1 stick) butter, softened
⅓ cup plus 2 teaspoons rum, divided
⅓ cup water
1 quart spumone ice cream, softened
1 cup whipping cream
1 tablespoon powdered sugar
Candied cherries
Red and green decorating sugars (optional)

1. Preheat oven to 375°F. Grease and flour 15×10-inch jelly-roll pan. Beat cake mix, eggs, butter, ⅓ cup rum and water in large bowl with electric mixer at low speed until moistened. Beat at high speed 4 minutes. Spread batter evenly in prepared pan.

2. Bake 20 to 25 minutes or until toothpick inserted into center comes out clean. Cool in pan 10 minutes. Remove to wire rack; cool completely.

3. Cut cake crosswise into three equal pieces. Place one cake layer on serving plate. Spread with half of ice cream. Repeat layers. Top with remaining cake layer; gently push down. Wrap and freeze at least 4 hours.

4. Just before serving, beat cream, powdered sugar and remaining 2 teaspoons rum in small bowl at high speed until stiff peaks form. Spread thin layer of whipped cream mixture over top of cake. Place star tip in pastry bag; fill with remaining whipped cream mixture. Pipe rosettes around top edges of cake. Place candied cherries in narrow strip down center of cake. Sprinkle decorating sugars over rosettes, if desired. Serve immediately. *Makes 8 to 10 servings*

Chocolate Peanut Butter Birthday Cake

1 package (about 18 ounces) devil's food cake mix, plus ingredients
    to prepare mix
1 package (about 11 ounces) peanut butter and chocolate chips
1 container (16 ounces) milk chocolate frosting
    Assorted fruit roll-ups
    Candles or thin pretzel sticks

1. Preheat oven to 350°F. Grease and flour two 8-inch round cake pans.

2. Prepare cake mix according to package directions; stir in ⅓ cup peanut butter and chocolate chips. Pour batter evenly into prepared pans.

3. Bake 30 minutes or until toothpick inserted into centers comes out clean. Cool completely in pans on wire racks.

4. Place one cake layer on serving plate; spread with ½ cup frosting. Top with remaining cake layer; frost cake with remaining frosting. Gently press remaining peanut butter and chocolate chips onto side of cake and around top edge.

5. To make decorative flags, cut triangles from fruit roll-ups. Make two ½- to ¾-inch horizontal cuts along short side of one triangle. Weave one candle in and out of cuts. Repeat with remaining triangles and candles. Arrange flags on cake.   *Makes 12 servings*

Note: Flags can be decorated with the birthday child's name or the name of each guest attending the party using decorating icing.

Butter Brickle Cake

⅔ cup sugar
2 teaspoons ground cinnamon
1 package (about 18 ounces) yellow cake mix
1 package (4-serving size) butterscotch instant pudding and pie filling mix
4 eggs
¾ cup vegetable oil
¾ cup water
1 cup chopped walnuts, divided

1. Preheat oven to 350°F. Grease and flour 13×9-inch baking pan. Combine sugar and cinnamon in small bowl.

2. Beat cake mix, pudding mix, eggs, oil and water in large bowl with electric mixer at medium speed 5 minutes or until fluffy. Pour half of batter into prepared baking pan. Sprinkle with ½ cup walnuts and half of sugar mixture. Top with remaining batter. Sprinkle with remaining walnuts and sugar mixture.

3. Bake 40 minutes or until toothpick inserted into center comes out clean. Cool completely in pan on wire rack.   *Makes 12 to 15 servings*

Serving Suggestion: This cake is great served warm. Try topping it with whipped cream or vanilla ice cream for a special treat.

 *Casual Cakes*

Cranberry Chocolate Cake

    1 package (about 18 ounces) devil's food cake mix
1⅓ cups water
    3 eggs
  ½ cup vegetable oil
    1 can (16 ounces) whole berry cranberry sauce, divided
    1 container (8 ounces) whipped topping
    2 tablespoons cocoa powder
    1 cup sliced almonds, toasted*

To toast almonds, spread in single layer on baking sheet. Bake in preheated 350°F oven 5 to 7 minutes or until golden brown, stirring occasionally.

1. Preheat oven to 350°F. Grease bottom of 13×9-inch baking pan.

2. Beat cake mix, water, eggs and oil in large bowl with electric mixer at medium speed until blended. Add half of cranberry sauce; beat until well blended. Pour batter into prepared baking pan.

3. Bake 30 minutes or until toothpick inserted into center comes out clean. Cool completely in pan on wire rack.

4. Place whipped topping in medium bowl. Fold in cocoa.

5. Place remaining cranberry sauce in small microwavable bowl; heat on HIGH 15 seconds or until softened. Spread evenly over cake. Top with whipped topping mixture. Cover and refrigerate until serving. Sprinkle with almonds.

Makes 12 to 15 servings

 *Casual Cakes*

Sweet Potato-Ginger Cake

    1 package (about 18 ounces) spice cake mix
1⅓ cups water
    1 cup mashed sweet potatoes (see Note)
    6 egg whites
    2 tablespoons canola oil
    1 tablespoon grated fresh ginger
    1 container (8 ounces) whipped topping

1. Preheat oven to 350°F. Coat 13×9-inch baking pan with nonstick cooking spray.

2. Combine cake mix, water, sweet potatoes, egg whites, oil and ginger in large bowl. Mix according to package directions. Pour batter into prepared baking pan.

3. Bake 30 minutes or until toothpick inserted into center comes out clean. Cool completely in pan on wire rack.

4. Frost with whipped topping. Cover and refrigerate until serving.

Makes 12 to 15 servings

Note: 1 can (15 ounces) sweet potatoes in syrup, drained and mashed, equals about 1 cup.

 *Casual Cakes*

Chocolate Crispy Treat Cake

- 1 package (about 18 ounces) chocolate fudge cake mix, plus ingredients to prepare mix
- 1 cup semisweet chocolate chips
- ¼ cup light corn syrup
- ¼ cup (½ stick) butter
- ½ cup powdered sugar
- 2 cups crisp rice cereal
- 4 cups mini marshmallows (half of 10½-ounce package)

1. Preheat oven to 350°F. Grease bottom of 13×9-inch baking pan. Prepare cake mix according to package directions. Pour batter into prepared baking pan.

2. Bake 30 minutes or until toothpick inserted into center comes out almost clean.

3. Meanwhile, heat chocolate chips, corn syrup and butter in large saucepan over low heat, stirring frequently, until chocolate and butter are melted. Remove from heat; stir in powdered sugar. Gently stir in cereal until well blended.

4. Sprinkle marshmallows over top of cake. Bake 2 to 3 minutes or until marshmallows puff up slightly.

5. Spread chocolate cereal mixture over marshmallows. Let stand until set.

Makes 12 to 15 servings

TIP

This cake is best eaten within a day or two of baking. The cereal will become soggy if the cake sits any longer. Luckily, it is so delicious that it rarely lasts that long.

 *Casual Cakes*

Tres Leches Cake

1 package (about 18 ounces) white cake mix, plus ingredients
    to prepare mix
1 can (14 ounces) sweetened condensed milk
1 cup milk
1 cup whipping cream
1 container (8 ounces) whipped topping
   Fresh fruit (optional)

1. Preheat oven to 350°F. Spray 13×9-inch baking pan with nonstick cooking spray.

2. Prepare cake mix according to package directions. Pour batter into prepared baking pan. Bake 30 minutes or until toothpick inserted into center comes out clean. Cool in pan 5 minutes.

3. Meanwhile, combine sweetened condensed milk, milk and whipping cream in 4-cup measure. Poke holes into warm cake with toothpick. Slowly pour milk mixture evenly over cake. Let stand 10 to 15 minutes to absorb liquid. Cover and refrigerate at least 1 hour.

4. Spread whipped topping over cake. Garnish with fruit. Cover and refrigerate until serving. *Makes 12 to 15 servings*

Rocky Road Cake

1 cup chopped walnuts or pecans
1 package (about 18 ounces) devil's food cake mix
1⅓ cups water
3 eggs
½ cup vegetable oil
2 teaspoons instant coffee granules (optional)
4 cups mini marshmallows
1 container (16 ounces) hot fudge topping

1. Preheat oven to 350°F. Grease 13×9-inch baking pan.

2. Toast walnuts in medium skillet over medium-high heat 5 minutes or just until beginning to brown, stirring frequently. Remove from heat; cool completely.

3. Beat cake mix, water, eggs, oil and coffee granules, if desired, in large bowl with electric mixer at low speed 1 minute or until well blended. Pour batter into prepared baking pan.

4. Bake 30 minutes or until toothpick inserted into center comes out almost clean. Immediately sprinkle marshmallows over cake; top with walnuts. Cool in pan 15 minutes.

5. Heat hot fudge topping in microwave according to package directions. Drizzle evenly over cake. Cool completely. *Makes 12 to 15 servings*

Carrot Snack Cake

- 1 package (about 18 ounces) butter recipe yellow cake mix with pudding in the mix, plus ingredients to prepare mix
- 2 jars (4 ounces each) strained carrot baby food
- 1½ cups chopped walnuts, divided
- 1 cup shredded carrots
- ½ cup golden raisins
- 1½ teaspoons ground cinnamon
- 1½ teaspoons vanilla, divided
- 1 package (8 ounces) cream cheese, softened
  Grated peel of 1 lemon
- 2 teaspoons lemon juice
- 3 cups powdered sugar

1. Preheat oven to 350°F. Grease 13×9-inch baking pan.

2. Prepare cake mix according to package directions, using ½ cup water instead of amount called for in directions. Stir in carrot baby food, 1 cup walnuts, carrots, raisins, cinnamon and ½ teaspoon vanilla. Spread batter in prepared baking pan.

3. Bake 40 minutes or until toothpick inserted into center comes out clean. Cool completely in pan on wire rack.

4. Beat cream cheese in large bowl with electric mixer at medium speed until fluffy. Beat in lemon peel, lemon juice and remaining 1 teaspoon vanilla. Gradually add powdered sugar; beat until well blended and smooth. Spread frosting over cake; sprinkle with remaining ½ cup walnuts. Refrigerate 2 hours before serving.   *Makes 12 to 24 servings*

German Upside-Down Cake

1½ cups shredded coconut
1 cup chopped pecans
1 container (16 ounces) coconut pecan frosting
1 package (about 18 ounces) German chocolate cake mix
1⅓ cups water
4 eggs
1 cup milk chocolate chips
⅓ cup vegetable oil
Whipped cream (optional)

1. Preheat oven to 350°F. Spray 13×9-inch glass baking dish with nonstick cooking spray.

2. Spread coconut evenly in prepared baking dish. Sprinkle pecans over coconut. Spoon frosting by tablespoonfuls over pecans. (Do not spread.)

3. Beat cake mix, water, eggs, chocolate chips and oil in large bowl with electric mixer at low speed 30 seconds. Beat at medium speed 2 minutes or until well blended and creamy. Pour batter into prepared pan, spreading lightly over frosting.

4. Bake 35 minutes or until toothpick inserted into center comes out clean. Cool in pan 10 minutes. Invert onto serving plate; serve warm. Top with whipped cream, if desired.   *Makes 12 to 15 servings*

 *Casual Cakes*

Caribbean Cake Squares

1 package (9 ounces) yellow cake mix
½ cup orange juice
2 egg whites
2 cans (8 ounces each) crushed pineapple in juice
   Additional orange juice
1 tablespoon cornstarch
½ cup slivered almonds
½ cup shredded coconut
2 large ripe bananas
1 can (15 ounces) mandarin orange segments in light syrup, drained

1. Preheat oven to 350°F. Spray 13×9-inch baking pan with nonstick cooking spray.

2. Beat cake mix, ½ cup orange juice and egg whites in medium bowl with electric mixer at medium speed until well blended. Pour batter evenly into prepared baking pan.

3. Bake 12 minutes or until toothpick inserted into center comes out clean. Cool completely in pan on wire rack.

4. Drain juice from pineapple into 2-cup measure; reserve crushed pineapple. Add additional orange juice to measure 1½ cups liquid. Stir in cornstarch until smooth. Bring juice mixture to a boil in medium saucepan over high heat, stirring constantly. Boil 1 minute, stirring constantly. Remove from heat.

5. Toast almonds and coconut in large skillet over medium heat until golden brown, stirring frequently.

6. Spread pineapple evenly over cake. Slice bananas and arrange over pineapple. Top with mandarin oranges. Drizzle juice mixture evenly over top. Sprinkle with almond mixture. Cover and refrigerate 1 to 4 hours.

Makes 12 to 15 servings

 Casual Cakes

Double Chocolate Chip Snack Cake

1 package (about 18 ounces) devil's food cake mix with pudding
    in the mix, divided
2 eggs
½ cup water
¼ cup vegetable oil
½ teaspoon cinnamon
1 cup semisweet chocolate chips, divided
¼ cup packed brown sugar
2 tablespoons butter, melted
¾ cup white chocolate chips

1. Preheat oven to 350°F. Grease 9-inch round cake pan. Reserve ¾ cup dry cake mix.

2. Beat remaining cake mix, eggs, water, oil and cinnamon in large bowl with electric mixer at medium speed 2 minutes. Remove ½ cup batter; reserve for another use.* Spread remaining batter in prepared pan; sprinkle with ½ cup semisweet chocolate chips.

3. Combine reserved dry cake mix and brown sugar in medium bowl. Stir in butter and remaining ½ cup semisweet chocolate chips. Sprinkle over batter in pan.

4. Bake 35 minutes or until toothpick inserted into center comes out clean. Cool in pan 10 minutes. Remove to wire rack; cool completely.

5. Place white chocolate chips in medium resealable food storage bag; seal bag. Microwave on HIGH 10 seconds and knead bag gently. Repeat until chips are melted. Cut off ¼ inch from corner of bag; drizzle chocolate over cake. Let stand until set. *Makes 8 to 10 servings*

If desired, extra batter can be used for cupcakes. Pour batter into two foil baking cups placed on baking sheet. Bake at 350°F 18 minutes or until toothpick inserted into centers comes out clean.

Crunchy Peach Snack Cake

1 package (9 ounces) yellow cake mix
1 container (6 ounces) peach yogurt
1 egg
¼ cup peach fruit spread
¾ cup square whole grain oat cereal with cinnamon,
    slightly crushed
Whipped cream (optional)

1. Place oven rack in center of oven. Preheat oven to 350°F. Lightly grease 8-inch square baking pan.

2. Beat cake mix, yogurt and egg in medium bowl with electric mixer at low speed until blended. Beat at medium speed 2 minutes or until smooth.

3. Spread batter evenly in prepared baking pan. Drop fruit spread by ½ teaspoonfuls over top. Sprinkle with cereal.

4. Bake 25 minutes or until toothpick inserted into center comes out clean. Cool completely in pan on wire rack. Serve with whipped cream, if desired.

Makes 9 servings

Topsy-Turvy Banana Crunch Cake

⅓ cup old-fashioned oats
3 tablespoons packed brown sugar
1 tablespoon all-purpose flour
¼ teaspoon ground cinnamon
2 tablespoons butter
2 tablespoons chopped pecans
1 package (9 ounces) yellow cake mix *without* pudding in the mix
½ cup sour cream
½ cup mashed banana (about 1 medium)
1 egg, slightly beaten
½ cup pecan pieces (optional)

1. Preheat oven to 350°F. Lightly grease 8-inch square baking pan.

2. Combine oats, brown sugar, flour and cinnamon in small bowl. Cut in butter with pastry blender or two knives until mixture resembles coarse crumbs. Stir in chopped pecans.

3. Beat cake mix, sour cream, banana and egg in medium bowl with electric mixer at low speed until blended. Beat at medium speed 2 minutes or until smooth. Spread half of batter evenly in prepared baking pan; sprinkle with half of oat mixture. Top with remaining batter and oat topping. Sprinkle with pecan pieces, if desired.

4. Bake 25 minutes or until toothpick inserted into center comes out clean. Cool completely in pan on wire rack. *Makes 9 servings*

Individual Flower Pot Cakes

18 (4×2½-inch) sterilized unglazed terra cotta pots (see Note)
1 package (about 18 ounces) dark chocolate cake mix, plus ingredients
    to prepare mix
1 package (12 ounces) semisweet chocolate chips
8 to 10 chocolate sandwich cookies, broken
1 container (16 ounces) chocolate frosting
    Green drinking straws
    Lollipops, decorating icing and assorted candies
    Spearmint leaves and gummy worms

1. Preheat oven to 350°F. Generously grease flower pots; line bottoms with greased parchment paper. Place pots in standard (2½-inch) muffin cups.

2. Prepare cake mix according to package directions; stir in chocolate chips. Spoon batter into pots, filling half full.

3. Bake 35 minutes or until toothpick inserted into centers comes out clean. Remove pots to wire racks; cool completely.

4. Place cookies in food processor; process using on/off pulsing action until coarse crumbs form.

5. Frost cakes with chocolate frosting. Sprinkle cookie crumbs over frosting to resemble dirt.

6. Push straws into each flower pot for stems; trim straws to different heights with scissors. Insert lollipops into straw stems. Decorate lollipops with decorating icing and assorted candies. Arrange spearmint leaves and gummy worms around base of lollipop flowers. *Makes 18 cakes*

Note: The terra cotta pots used in this recipe should be new and never used for gardening. They can be found in garden centers and hardware stores. To sterilize the pots before preparing these cakes, wash them thoroughly and allow to dry completely. Bake in a preheated 350°F oven for 3 hours. Remove to wire racks; cool completely.

Mini Neapolitan Ice Cream Cakes

1 package (about 18 ounces) vanilla cake mix
¾ cup water
3 eggs
⅓ cup vegetable oil
⅓ cup unsweetened cocoa powder
4 cups slightly softened strawberry ice cream
  Powdered sugar, dark chocolate curls and strawberries (optional)

1. Preheat oven to 350°F. Spray 4 mini (5×3-inch) loaf pans with nonstick cooking spray.

2. Beat cake mix, water, eggs and oil in large bowl with electric mixer at low speed 30 seconds. Beat at medium speed 2 minutes or until well blended. Reserve 1¾ cups batter. Add cocoa to remaining batter; stir until well blended.

3. Divide chocolate batter evenly between 2 prepared pans. Divide reserved plain batter evenly between remaining 2 prepared pans.

4. Bake 30 minutes or until toothpick inserted into centers comes out clean. Cool in pans 10 minutes. Remove to wire racks; cool completely.

5. Trim rounded tops of cakes with serrated knife. Cut each cake in half horizontally. Line 4 clean mini loaf pans with plastic wrap, leaving 2-inch overhang on all sides. Place 1 vanilla cake layer in each pan.

6. Place ice cream in large bowl; beat with electric mixer at medium speed 30 seconds or just until spreadable. Spread 1 cup ice cream over each vanilla cake layer in pans; top with chocolate cake layers. Cover tops of cakes with plastic wrap. Freeze at least 4 hours.

7. Remove cakes from loaf pans; trim any uneven sides. To serve, cut each cake into thirds. Garnish with powdered sugar, chocolate curls and strawberries.

Makes 12 servings

 *Sweet Miniatures*

Dark Chocolate Lava Cakes

1½ cups milk
1 package (4-serving size) chocolate instant pudding and pie filling mix
1 package (about 18 ounces) dark chocolate cake mix
1 cup buttermilk
2 eggs
3 egg yolks
¼ cup vegetable oil
2 tablespoons water
1 tablespoon butter, melted
¼ cup granulated sugar
Powdered sugar

1. Combine milk and pudding mix in medium bowl; whisk until smooth. Place plastic wrap on surface of pudding; refrigerate.

2. Combine cake mix, buttermilk, eggs, egg yolks, oil and water in large bowl until almost smooth. (Do not use electric mixer.) Cover and refrigerate 1 hour.

3. Preheat oven to 400°F. Brush 14 (5-ounce) custard cups with butter. Coat evenly with granulated sugar.

4. Spoon 2 tablespoons batter into each prepared custard cup. Bake 10 to 12 minutes (batter will not cook through completely). Remove cups from oven; place 1 heaping tablespoon pudding in center of each cup and top with 2 tablespoons batter.

5. Bake 14 to 16 minutes or until toothpick inserted in top layer of cakes comes out clean. Cool in cups 7 to 10 minutes. Invert cakes onto plates. Sprinkle with powdered sugar. Serve immediately. *Makes 14 cakes*

Kelly Green Mini Bundt Cakes

2 tablespoons butter, melted
1 package (about 18 ounces) white cake mix, plus ingredients
    to prepare mix
  Green food coloring
1 container (16 ounces) white frosting
  Green decorating sugar

1. Preheat oven to 350°F. Brush 12 small (1-cup) bundt pan cups with butter.

2. Prepare cake mix according to package directions. Add food coloring to batter, a few drops at a time, until desired shade of green is reached. Fill prepared bundt cups half full.

3. Bake 20 minutes or until toothpick inserted near centers comes out clean. Cool in pans 10 minutes. Remove to wire racks; cool completely.

4. Place frosting in medium microwavable bowl. Add food coloring, one drop at a time, until desired shade is reached. Microwave on LOW (30%) 30 seconds or until pourable but not melted. Spoon frosting over cakes. Sprinkle with decorating sugar. *Makes 12 cakes*

Whoopie Pies

1 package (about 18 ounces) devil's food cake mix *without* pudding in the mix
1 package (4-serving size) chocolate instant pudding and pie filling mix
1¼ cups (2½ sticks) butter, softened, divided
4 eggs
1 cup water
1¼ cups marshmallow creme
¾ cup powdered sugar
½ teaspoon vanilla

1. Preheat oven to 350°F. Grease baking sheets.

2. Beat cake mix, pudding mix, ½ cup butter, eggs and water in large bowl with electric mixer at low speed just until moistened. Beat at medium speed 2 minutes or until light and thick. Drop batter by heaping tablespoonfuls 2 inches apart onto prepared baking sheets.

3. Bake 12 to 14 minutes or until cakes spring back when lightly touched. Cool on baking sheets 5 minutes. Remove to wire racks; cool completely.

4. For filling, beat remaining ¾ cup butter, marshmallow creme, powdered sugar and vanilla in large bowl at high speed 2 minutes or until light and fluffy.

5. Spread filling on flat sides of half of cakes; top with remaining cakes.

Makes 2 dozen servings

Red Velvet Hearts

1 package (about 18 ounces) red velvet cake mix
¾ cup (1½ sticks) butter, softened
2 eggs
1 cup chopped pecans (optional)
1 container (16 ounces) cream cheese frosting
Assorted red decors and candies

1. Preheat oven 350°F. Line 13×9-inch baking pan with foil, leaving 1-inch overhang on all sides. Spray foil with nonstick cooking spray.

2. Beat cake mix, butter and eggs in large bowl with electric mixer at medium speed 1 minute. (Mixture will be thick.) Add pecans, if desired; beat just until combined. Spread batter evenly in prepared baking pan.

3. Bake 25 minutes or until toothpick inserted into center comes out almost clean. Cool completely in pan on wire rack.

4. Cut out hearts with 3-inch cookie cutter. Spread frosting over hearts; decorate with decors and candies. Store covered in refrigerator.

Makes about 2 dozen hearts

Cran-Lemon Coffee Cakes

1 package (about 18 ounces) yellow cake mix with pudding in the mix
1 cup water
3 eggs
⅓ cup butter, melted and cooled
¼ cup lemon juice
1 tablespoon grated lemon peel
1½ cups coarsely chopped cranberries
   Lemon Glaze (recipe follows)
   Additional grated lemon peel (optional)

1. Preheat oven to 350°F. Grease and flour 9 small (1-cup) bundt pan cups. Beat cake mix, water, eggs, butter, lemon juice and 1 tablespoon lemon peel in large bowl with electric mixer at low speed 2 minutes. Fold in cranberries. Pour batter into prepared bundt cups, filling two-thirds full.

2. Bake 20 minutes or until toothpick inserted near centers comes out clean. Cool in pans 10 minutes. Remove to wire racks; cool completely.

3. Prepare Lemon Glaze; drizzle over cakes. Garnish with additional grated lemon peel. Let stand until set.   *Makes 9 cakes*

Lemon Glaze: Beat 1 cup powdered sugar and 3 tablespoons lemon juice in small bowl until well blended.

Circus Train Mini Cakes

1 package (about 18 ounces) chocolate fudge cake mix
1⅓ cups water
3 eggs
½ cup vegetable oil
2 containers (16 ounces each) chocolate frosting
2 round candy wafers
   Candy-coated chocolate pieces
   Licorice snap
   Round mints, assorted colors
   Iced animal crackers

1. Preheat oven to 350°F. Spray 6 mini (4×2-inch) foil loaf pans and one foil baking cup with nonstick cooking spray.

2. Beat cake mix, water, eggs and oil in large bowl with electric mixer at low speed 30 seconds. Beat at medium speed 2 minutes or until blended. Pour batter into prepared pans, filling two-thirds full.

3. Bake 13 to 15 minutes or until toothpick inserted into centers comes out clean. Cool completely in pans on wire racks.

4. Place engine car at front edge of large platter. Line up train cars behind engine. Frost cars, using bottom of each loaf as top. Place cupcake upside down on top of engine car, lining it up with rear of car; frost cupcake.

5. Use wafers and chocolate pieces for eyes and mouth on engine. Use licorice snap for smokestack. Attach mints to each car for wheels. Attach another mint to back of last car for taillight. Place animal crackers on tops of cars. To serve, remove top of engine car and cut each train car in half. *Makes 13 servings*

Lemony Cake Critters

1 package (about 18 ounces) lemon cake mix
½ cup all-purpose flour
2 eggs
⅓ cup vegetable oil
 Grated peel of 1 lemon
1 container (16 ounces) cream cheese frosting
 Assorted food colorings, colored sprinkles or sugar, candy-coated
  chocolate pieces and flaked coconut (optional)

1. Preheat oven to 350°F. Spray baking sheets with nonstick cooking spray.

2. Beat cake mix, flour, eggs, oil and lemon peel in large bowl with electric mixer at low speed until well blended. Roll out dough between parchment paper to ½-inch thickness. Cut out shapes using 2-inch cookie cutters. Place 1 inch apart on prepared baking sheets.

3. Bake 10 to 12 minutes or until light brown. Cool on baking sheets 5 minutes. Remove to wire racks; cool completely.

4. Tint frosting with food coloring, if desired. Frost cookies and decorate as desired.   *Makes about 16 critters*

Jingle Bells Ice Cream Sandwiches

1 package (about 18 ounces) devil's food cake mix
5 tablespoons butter, melted
3 eggs
50 hard peppermint candies, unwrapped
1 quart vanilla ice cream

1. Preheat oven to 350°F. Spray baking sheets with nonstick cooking spray.

2. Beat cake mix, butter and eggs in large bowl with electric mixer at medium speed until blended and smooth. Drop dough by rounded tablespoonfuls 2 inches apart onto prepared baking sheets.

3. Bake 12 minutes or until edges are set and centers are no longer shiny. Cool on baking sheets 5 minutes. Remove to wire racks; cool completely.

4. Place peppermint candies in medium resealable food storage bag. Seal bag; crush candies with rolling pin or back of small skillet. Place crushed candies in shallow bowl. Line shallow baking pan with waxed paper.

5. Place scoop of ice cream on flat sides of half of cookies. Top with remaining cookies. Roll edges in crushed peppermints; place in prepared baking pan. Cover and freeze until ready to serve. *Makes about 1½ dozen sandwiches*

Prep Time: 25 minutes
Bake Time: 12 minutes

Apple-Walnut Glazed Spice Baby Cakes

1 package (about 18 ounces) spice cake mix
1⅓ cups plus 3 tablespoons water, divided
3 eggs
⅓ cup vegetable oil
½ teaspoon vanilla, butter and nut flavoring*
¾ cup chopped walnuts
12 ounces Granny Smith apples, peeled and cut into ½-inch cubes (about 3 medium)
¼ teaspoon ground cinnamon
1 jar (12 ounces) caramel ice cream topping

Vanilla, butter and nut flavoring is available in the baking aisles of most large supermarkets.

1. Preheat oven to 350°F. Grease and flour 12 small (1-cup) bundt pan cups.

2. Beat cake mix, 1⅓ cups water, eggs, oil and flavoring in large bowl with electric mixer at low speed 30 seconds. Beat at medium speed 2 minutes. Spoon batter evenly into prepared bundt cups.

3. Bake 25 minutes or until toothpick inserted near centers comes out clean. Cool in pans 15 minutes. Remove to wire racks; cool completely.

4. Meanwhile, place large skillet over medium heat. Add walnuts; cook and stir 3 minutes or until lightly browned. Transfer to small bowl. Add apples, remaining 3 tablespoons water and cinnamon to skillet; cook and stir 3 minutes or until apples are crisp-tender. Remove from heat; stir in walnuts and caramel topping. Spoon apple mixture over cakes.   *Makes 12 cakes*

Citrusy Pound Cakes

2 packages (16 ounces each) pound cake mix
4 eggs
1 cup water
½ cup orange juice
2 tablespoons lemon juice
2 teaspoons grated lemon peel
2 teaspoons grated orange peel
Citrus Glaze (recipe follows)

1. Preheat oven to 350°F. Spray 6 mini (5×3-inch) loaf pans with nonstick cooking spray. Place on baking sheet.

2. Whisk cake mix, eggs, water, orange juice, lemon juice, lemon peel and orange peel in large bowl 2 minutes or until combined. Pour 1 cup batter into each prepared loaf pan.

3. Bake 45 minutes or until toothpick inserted into centers comes out clean. Cool completely in pans on wire racks.

4. Prepare Citrus Glaze. Drizzle over loaves; let stand until set.

Makes 6 mini loaves

Citrus Glaze

1 cup powdered sugar
1 tablespoon orange or lemon juice
½ teaspoon vanilla (optional)

Combine powdered sugar, orange juice and vanilla, if desired, in small bowl. Mix well. Add more juice, if necessary, to reach desired consistency.

Makes ½ cup

Quick Triple-Chocolate Cake

1 package (about 18 ounces) chocolate cake mix *without* pudding in the mix
1 package (4-serving size) chocolate instant pudding and pie filling mix
1 cup sour cream
4 eggs
½ cup vegetable or canola oil
½ cup water
1 cup semisweet chocolate chips or chunks
Powdered sugar (optional)

1. Preheat oven to 350°F. Spray 12-cup bundt pan with nonstick cooking spray.

2. Beat cake mix, pudding mix, sour cream, eggs, oil and water in large bowl with electric mixer at low speed 1 minute. Beat at medium speed 2 minutes or until well blended. Stir in chocolate chips. Pour into prepared pan.

3. Bake 50 minutes or until toothpick inserted near center comes out clean. Cool in pan 10 minutes. Remove to wire rack; cool completely. Sprinkle with powdered sugar, if desired.   *Makes 18 servings*

Prep Time: 10 minutes
Bake Time: 50 minutes

Lemon-Cherry Coffee Cake

  2 packages (9 ounces each) yellow cake mix
½ cup (1 stick) cold butter, cut into pieces
¼ cup buttermilk
  1 egg
  1 teaspoon vanilla
  1 teaspoon grated lemon or orange peel
½ cup dried cherries or cranberries
  1 egg white
½ teaspoon water
  1 tablespoon sugar
½ cup sliced almonds

1. Preheat oven to 350°F. Spray 9-inch springform pan with nonstick cooking spray.

2. Place cake mix in large bowl. Cut in butter using pastry blender or two knives until well blended. Stir in buttermilk, egg, vanilla and lemon peel until blended. Fold in cherries. (Batter will be sticky.) Spread batter evenly in prepared pan.

3. Beat egg white and water in small bowl; brush over top of batter. Sprinkle with sugar. Score into eight wedges with knife. Sprinkle with almonds.

4. Bake 20 to 25 minutes or until toothpick inserted into center comes out clean. Immediately cut into wedges along score lines. Cool in pan on wire rack 10 minutes. Remove side and base of pan. Serve warm.   *Makes 8 servings*

Easy Apple Butter Cake

1 package (about 18 ounces) yellow cake mix *without* pudding in the mix
1 package (4-serving size) vanilla instant pudding and pie filling mix
1 cup sour cream
1 cup apple butter
4 eggs
½ cup apple juice
¼ cup vegetable oil
1 teaspoon ground cinnamon
½ teaspoon ground nutmeg
½ teaspoon ground cloves
¼ teaspoon salt
   Powdered sugar

1. Preheat oven to 375°F. Spray 10-inch tube pan with nonstick cooking spray.

2. Beat cake mix, pudding mix, sour cream, apple butter, eggs, apple juice, oil, cinnamon, nutmeg, cloves and salt in large bowl with electric mixer at low speed 1 minute. Beat at medium speed 2 minutes or until well blended and fluffy. Pour batter into prepared pan.

3. Bake 45 minutes or until toothpick inserted near center comes out clean. Cool in pan on wire rack 20 minutes. Run sharp knife along edge of pan to release cake; invert cake onto serving plate. Cool completely.

4. Just before serving, place 9-inch paper doily over cake. Sift powdered sugar over doily; carefully remove doily.   *Makes 12 servings*

Mandarin Orange Tea Cake

1 package (16 ounces) pound cake mix
½ cup plus 2 tablespoons orange juice, divided
2 eggs
¼ cup milk
1 can (15 ounces) mandarin orange segments in light syrup, drained
¾ cup powdered sugar
   Grated peel of 1 orange

1. Preheat oven to 350°F. Grease 9-inch bundt pan.

2. Beat cake mix, ½ cup orange juice, eggs and milk in large bowl with electric mixer at medium speed 2 minutes or until light and fluffy. Fold in orange segments. Pour batter into prepared pan.

3. Bake 45 minutes or until golden brown and toothpick inserted near center comes out clean. Cool in pan 15 minutes. Invert cake onto wire rack; cool completely.

4. Combine sugar, orange peel and remaining 2 tablespoons orange juice in small bowl; stir until smooth. Drizzle over cake; let stand until set.

Makes 16 servings

Sweet and Sour Brunch Cake

1 package (16 ounces) frozen rhubarb, thawed and patted dry
1 cup packed brown sugar
1 tablespoon all-purpose flour
1 teaspoon ground cinnamon
¼ cup (½ stick) butter, cut into small pieces
1 package (about 18 ounces) yellow cake mix *without* pudding in the mix
1 package (4-serving size) vanilla instant pudding and pie filling mix
4 eggs
⅔ cup sour cream
½ cup water
½ cup vegetable oil

1. Preheat oven to 350°F. Spray 13×9-inch baking pan with nonstick cooking spray.

2. Spread rhubarb evenly in single layer in prepared baking pan. Combine brown sugar, flour and cinnamon in small bowl; mix well. Sprinkle evenly over rhubarb; dot with butter.

3. Beat cake mix, pudding mix, eggs, sour cream, water and oil in large bowl with electric mixer at low speed 1 minute. Beat at medium speed 2 minutes or until well blended. Spread over rhubarb mixture.

4. Bake 40 minutes or until toothpick inserted into center comes out clean. Cool in pan 5 minutes. Invert onto serving plate. Serve warm or at room temperature.

Makes 16 to 18 servings

Note: If frozen rhubarb is unavailable, you may substitute frozen unsweetened strawberries.

Chai Spice Cake

2¼ cups water
10 chai tea bags
1 cup ice cubes
1 package (about 18 ounces) white cake mix
3 egg whites
⅓ cup vegetable oil
1 tablespoon cornstarch
¼ cup packed brown sugar
6 whole cloves
½ teaspoon vanilla

1. Preheat oven to 350°F. Spray bottom of 10- or 12-cup nonstick bundt pan with nonstick cooking spray.

2. Bring water to a boil in medium saucepan over high heat. Remove from heat; add tea bags. Steep 5 minutes. Remove and discard tea bags. Add ice cubes to saucepan; let stand until ice is completely melted. (This should make about 2¼ cups tea.)

3. Beat cake mix, 1¼ cups tea, egg whites and oil in large bowl with electric mixer at low speed 30 seconds. Beat at medium speed 2 minutes or until well blended. Pour batter into prepared pan. Bake according to package directions or until toothpick inserted near center comes out clean. Invert pan onto wire rack; let stand 10 minutes before removing pan. Cool completely.

4. Meanwhile, whisk cornstarch into remaining 1 cup tea in medium saucepan until smooth. Add brown sugar and cloves; bring to a boil over medium-high heat, stirring constantly. Cook and stir 1 minute. Cool completely. Remove and discard cloves. Stir in vanilla. Pour glaze evenly over cake; let stand until set.

Makes 16 servings

Fresh Fruit Tart

1 package (about 18 ounces) butter recipe yellow cake mix
½ cup (1 stick) butter, melted and cooled
2 eggs
1 teaspoon vanilla
⅓ cup apricot jam
1½ cups whipped topping
2 cups sliced strawberries
1 kiwi, peeled and sliced
⅓ cup blueberries

1. Preheat oven to 350°F. Spray 10-inch springform pan with nonstick cooking spray.

2. Beat cake mix, butter, eggs and vanilla in large bowl with electric mixer at low speed 2 minutes. (Batter will be very thick.) Spoon batter into prepared pan. Pat down top of batter with oiled fingers to flatten slightly.

3. Bake 25 minutes or until toothpick inserted into center comes out clean. Cool completely in pan on wire rack. Remove side and base of pan; slide crust onto serving plate.

4. Heat apricot jam in small microwavable bowl on HIGH 30 seconds or until jam is thin and syrupy.

5. Spread whipped topping evenly over crust. Arrange fruit decoratively over topping. Brush fruit with melted jam. Refrigerate leftovers. *Makes 8 servings*

Pecan Praline Brandy Cake

1 package (about 18 ounces) butter pecan cake mix
¾ cup water
⅓ cup plain yogurt
2 egg whites
1 egg
¼ cup plus ½ teaspoon brandy, divided
2 tablespoons vegetable oil
1 cup chopped toasted pecans, divided
⅔ cup packed light brown sugar
⅓ cup light corn syrup
¼ cup whipping cream
2 tablespoons butter
½ teaspoon vanilla

1. Preheat oven to 350°F. Spray 10- or 12-cup bundt pan with nonstick cooking spray.

2. Beat cake mix, water, yogurt, egg whites, egg, ¼ cup brandy and oil in medium bowl with electric mixer at low speed 30 seconds. Beat at medium speed 2 minutes or until light and fluffy. Fold in ½ cup pecans. Pour batter into prepared pan.

3. Bake 50 minutes or until toothpick inserted near center comes out clean. Cool in pan 10 minutes. Remove to wire rack; cool completely.

4. Combine brown sugar, corn syrup, cream and butter in small saucepan. Bring to a boil over medium heat, stirring constantly. Remove from heat; stir in remaining ½ cup pecans, ½ teaspoon brandy and vanilla. Cool to room temperature. Pour evenly over top of cake; let stand until set.

Makes 12 servings

Chocolate Cherry Coffee Cake

2 packages (about 17 ounces each) cinnamon swirl coffee cake mix
¾ cup chopped pecans
1½ cups water
4 eggs
⅓ cup vegetable oil
1¼ cups mini semisweet chocolate chips
1 can (20 ounces) cherry pie filling

1. Preheat oven to 350°F. Set aside glaze packets from mixes. Generously grease and flour 12-cup bundt pan.

2. Combine cinnamon streusel packets and pecans in small bowl. Sprinkle 1 cup mixture into bottom of prepared pan. Combine cake mixes, water, eggs and oil in large bowl; mix according to package directions. Gently stir in chocolate chips. Spread half of batter evenly over pecan mixture.

3. Drain cherry pie filling. (Do not rinse cherries.) Spoon cherries evenly over batter; sprinkle remaining cinnamon streusel mixture over cherries. Top with remaining batter.

4. Bake 45 minutes or until toothpick inserted near center comes out clean. Cool in pan 1 hour. Remove to wire rack; cool completely.

5. Prepare glaze packets according to package directions. Drizzle evenly over cake; let stand until set. *Makes 12 to 16 servings*

Zucchini Spice Bundt Cake

1 package (about 18 ounces) spice or carrot cake mix
1 cup water
3 eggs
2 tablespoons vegetable oil
1 zucchini, shredded
3 tablespoons chopped walnuts, toasted*
¾ teaspoon vanilla
¼ cup powdered sugar
1 to 2 teaspoons milk

To toast walnuts, spread in single layer on baking sheet. Bake in preheated 350°F oven 5 minutes or until golden brown, stirring frequently.

1. Preheat oven to 325°F. Spray 12-cup bundt pan with nonstick cooking spray.

2. Combine cake mix, water, eggs and oil in large bowl; mix according to package directions. Stir in zucchini, walnuts and vanilla until well blended. Pour into prepared pan.

3. Bake 40 minutes or until toothpick inserted near center comes out almost clean. Cool in pan 10 minutes. Remove to wire rack; cool completely.

4. Combine powdered sugar and milk in small bowl; stir until smooth. Drizzle evenly over cake; let stand until set.   *Makes 18 servings*

Table of Contents

Margarita Cupcakes

    1 package (about 18 ounces) white cake mix
    ¾ cup plus 2 tablespoons margarita mix, divided
    2 eggs
    ⅓ cup vegetable oil
    ¼ cup water
    3 teaspoons grated lime peel, divided
       Juice of 1 lime
    2 tablespoons tequila or lime juice
    3 cups powdered sugar
    1 tablespoon white decorating or granulated sugar
    1 tablespoon salt
       Green and yellow food coloring
       Lime peel strips (optional)

1. Preheat oven to 350°F. Line 24 standard (2½-inch) muffin cups with paper baking cups.

2. Whisk cake mix, ¾ cup margarita mix, eggs, oil, water, 1 teaspoon lime peel and lime juice in large bowl until well blended. Spoon batter evenly into prepared muffin cups.

3. Bake 20 minutes or until toothpick inserted into centers comes out clean. Cool in pans 10 minutes. Remove to wire racks; cool completely.

4. Combine tequila, remaining 2 tablespoons margarita mix and 2 teaspoons lime peel in medium bowl. Gradually whisk in powdered sugar. Combine decorating sugar and salt in small bowl. Add food coloring, one drop at a time, until desired shade of green is reached.

5. Spread glaze over cupcakes; dip edges in sugar-salt mixture. Garnish with lime peel strips.   *Makes 24 cupcakes*

Chai Latte Cupcakes

  7 chai tea bags, divided
1½ cups boiling water
  1 package (about 18 ounces) white cake mix
  3 eggs
⅓ cup vegetable oil
  1 cup milk
  2 to 3 cups powdered sugar
    Turbinado sugar (optional)

1. Place 4 tea bags in small bowl. Pour water over top; allow tea bags to steep until cooled slightly. Squeeze tea bags; discard.

2. Preheat oven to 350°F. Line 22 standard (2½-inch) muffin cups with paper baking cups.

3. Beat cake mix, tea, eggs and oil in large bowl with electric mixer at medium speed 2 minutes or until well blended. Spoon batter evenly into prepared muffin cups.

4. Bake 20 minutes or until toothpick inserted into centers comes out clean. Cool in pans 10 minutes. Remove to wire rack; cool completely.

5. Bring milk to a simmer in small saucepan over medium heat; remove from heat. Add remaining 3 tea bags; allow to steep until slightly cooled. Discard tea bags. Whisk in powdered sugar until smooth and thick enough for dipping.

6. Place wire rack over waxed paper. Dip tops of cupcakes in glaze; place on rack. Sprinkle with turbinado sugar, if desired. Let stand 10 minutes or until set.

Makes 22 cupcakes

Apple Cider Cupcakes

1 package (about 18 ounces) spice cake mix
1¼ cups apple cider
⅓ cup vegetable oil
3 eggs
2 cups coarsely chopped walnuts, plus additional for garnish
Apple Cider Frosting (recipe follows)

1. Preheat oven to 350°F. Line 24 standard (2½-inch) muffin cups with paper baking cups.

2. Beat cake mix, apple cider, oil and eggs in medium bowl with electric mixer at low speed until blended; beat at medium speed 2 minutes. Stir in 2 cups chopped walnuts. Spoon batter evenly into prepared muffin cups.

3. Bake 20 minutes or until toothpick inserted into centers comes out clean. Cool in pans 10 minutes. Remove to wire racks; cool completely.

4. Prepare Apple Cider Frosting; frost cupcakes. Garnish with additional chopped walnuts. *Makes 24 cupcakes*

Apple Cider Frosting: Beat ½ cup (1 stick) softened unsalted butter and ¼ cup apple cider in medium bowl with electric mixer at low speed until well blended. Gradually beat in 4 cups powdered sugar until smooth. Makes about 3 cups.

 Sugar and Spice

Cream-Filled Cupcakes

1 package (about 18 ounces) dark chocolate cake mix, plus ingredients
    to prepare mix
½ cup (1 stick) unsalted butter, softened
¼ cup shortening
3 cups powdered sugar
1⅓ cups whipping cream, divided
1 teaspoon salt
2 cups semisweet chocolate chips

1. Preheat oven to 350°F. Line 24 standard (2½-inch) muffin cups with paper baking cups. Prepare cake mix according to package directions. Spoon batter into prepared muffin cups, filling two-thirds full.

2. Bake 20 minutes or until toothpick inserted into centers comes out clean. Cool in pans 10 minutes. Remove to wire racks; cool completely.

3. Beat butter and shortening in large bowl with electric mixer at medium speed until well blended. Add powdered sugar, ⅓ cup cream and salt; beat at low speed 1 minute. Beat at medium-high speed 2 minutes or until fluffy. Place filling in pastry bag fitted with large round tip. Insert tip into top of each cupcake and squeeze in a small amount of filling. Reserve remaining filling.

4. Place chocolate chips in medium bowl. Bring remaining 1 cup cream to a simmer in small saucepan over medium heat. Pour cream over chocolate chips; let stand 1 minute. Whisk until chocolate is melted and mixture is smooth.

5. Place wire rack over waxed paper. Dip tops of cupcakes in chocolate mixture; place on rack. Dip a second time, if desired. Let stand until set. Pipe swirl design on top of chocolate using reserved filling. *Makes 24 cupcakes*

Peanut Butter & Jelly Cupcakes

1 package (about 18 ounces) yellow cake mix, plus ingredients
    to prepare mix
2 cups strawberry jelly
¾ cup creamy peanut butter
½ cup (1 stick) butter, softened
2 cups powdered sugar
½ teaspoon vanilla
¼ cup milk

1. Preheat oven to 350°F. Line 22 standard (2½-inch) muffin cups with paper baking cups. Prepare cake mix according to package directions. Spoon batter into prepared muffin cups, filling two-thirds full.

2. Bake 20 minutes or until toothpick inserted into centers comes out clean. Cool in pans 10 minutes. Remove to wire racks; cool completely.

3. Place jelly in pastry bag fitted with small round tip. Insert tip into tops of cupcakes; squeeze bag gently to fill centers with jelly.

4. Beat peanut butter and butter in medium bowl with electric mixer at medium speed until smooth. Add powdered sugar and vanilla; beat at low speed 1 minute or until crumbly. Slowly add milk, beating until creamy. Pipe or spread onto cupcakes. *Makes 22 cupcakes*

 Sugar and Spice

Angelic Cupcakes

1 package (about 16 ounces) angel food cake mix
1¼ cups cold water
¼ teaspoon peppermint extract (optional)
    Red food coloring
4½ cups whipped topping

1. Preheat oven to 375°F. Line 36 standard (2½-inch) muffin cups with paper baking cups.

2. Beat cake mix, water and peppermint extract, if desired, in large bowl with electric mixer at low speed 2 minutes. Pour half of batter into medium bowl; fold in nine drops red food coloring. Alternate spoonfuls of white and pink batter in each prepared muffin cup, filling three-fourths full.

3. Bake 11 minutes or until cupcakes are golden brown with deep cracks on top. Cool in pans 10 minutes. Remove to wire racks; cool completely.

4. Divide whipped topping between two small bowls. Add two drops red food coloring to one bowl; stir gently until whipped topping is evenly colored. Frost cupcakes with pink and white whipped topping as desired.

Makes 36 cupcakes

Angelic Cupcakes

 Sugar and Spice

Hot Chocolate Cupcakes

1 package (about 16 ounces) pound cake mix, plus ingredients
    to prepare mix
4 containers (4 ounces each) prepared chocolate pudding*
2½ cups whipped topping, divided
4 small chewy chocolate candies
    Unsweetened cocoa powder (optional)

*Or prepare 1 package (4-serving size) chocolate instant pudding and pie filling mix according to package directions. Use 2 cups pudding for recipe; reserve remaining pudding for another use.

1. Preheat oven to 350°F. Spray 15 standard (2½-inch) muffin cups with baking spray (nonstick cooking spray with flour added) or grease and flour cups. Prepare cake mix according to package directions. Spoon batter into prepared muffin cups, filling two-thirds full.

2. Bake 20 minutes or until toothpick inserted into centers comes out clean. Cool in pans 10 minutes. Remove to wire racks; cool completely.

3. Combine chocolate pudding and 2 cups whipped topping in medium bowl until well blended; refrigerate until ready to use.

4. Working with one at a time, unwrap chocolate candies and microwave on LOW (30%) 5 to 10 seconds or until slightly softened. Stretch into long thin rope; cut ropes into 2-inch lengths. Curve candy pieces for handles of mugs.

5. Cut 2-inch hole from top of each cupcake with small paring knife. Cut two slits, ½ inch apart, in one side of each cupcake. Insert chocolate candy into slits. Fill top of each cupcake with chocolate pudding mixture. Top with small dollop of remaining whipped topping; sprinkle with cocoa, if desired.

Makes 15 cupcakes

Lemon-Up Cakes

1 package (about 18 ounces) butter recipe yellow cake mix, plus ingredients
to prepare mix
Grated peel of 2 lemons, divided
½ cup lemon juice, divided
½ cup (1 stick) butter, softened
3½ cups powdered sugar
Yellow food coloring
1 package (9½ ounces) lemon-shaped hard candies, coarsely crushed

1. Preheat oven to 350°F. Grease 24 standard (2½-inch) muffin cups.

2. Prepare cake mix according to package directions using ¼ cup less water than indicated. Stir in half of lemon peel and ¼ cup lemon juice. Spoon batter evenly into prepared muffin cups.

3. Bake 20 minutes or until light golden brown and toothpick inserted into centers comes out clean. Cool in pans 5 minutes. Remove to wire racks; cool completely.

4. Beat butter in large bowl with electric mixer at medium speed until creamy. Gradually add powdered sugar; beat until blended. Add remaining lemon peel, ¼ cup lemon juice and several drops of food coloring; beat at medium speed until frosting is light and fluffy.

5. Frost cupcakes; sprinkle with crushed candies.   *Makes 24 cupcakes*

 Sugar and Spice

Black & Whites

1 package (about 18 ounces) vanilla cake mix, plus ingredients
     to prepare mix
⅔ cup semisweet chocolate chips, melted
4 ounces cream cheese, softened
1 cup prepared vanilla frosting
1 cup prepared chocolate frosting

1. Preheat oven to 350°F. Line 24 standard (2½-inch) muffin cups with paper baking cups.

2. Prepare cake mix according to package directions. Transfer half of batter (about 2½ cups) to medium bowl. Add melted chocolate and cream cheese to remaining batter; beat with electric mixer at medium speed 2 minutes or until smooth and well blended.

3. Spoon chocolate and vanilla batters side by side into prepared muffin cups, filling two-thirds full. (Use chocolate batter first as it is slightly thicker and easier to position on one side of muffin cups.)

4. Bake 16 minutes or until toothpick inserted into centers comes out clean. Cool in pans 10 minutes. Remove to wire racks; cool completely.

5. Spread vanilla frosting over half of each cupcake; spread chocolate frosting over remaining half of each cupcake.   *Makes 24 cupcakes*

 Sugar and Spice

Mini Doughnut Cupcakes

1 cup sugar
1½ teaspoons ground cinnamon
1 package (about 18 ounces) yellow or white cake mix, plus ingredients
    to prepare mix
1 tablespoon ground nutmeg

1. Preheat oven to 350°F. Grease and flour 60 mini (1¾-inch) muffin cups. Combine sugar and cinnamon in small bowl; set aside.

2. Prepare cake mix according to package directions; stir in nutmeg. Spoon batter into prepared muffin cups, filling two-thirds full.

3. Bake 12 minutes or until lightly browned and toothpick inserted into centers comes out clean.

4. Remove cupcakes from pans. Roll warm cupcakes in sugar mixture until completely coated. *Makes 60 mini cupcakes*

TIP

These irresistible little cupcakes allow you to enjoy the lightly spiced flavor of your favorite donuts without all the time and mess it takes to prepare and fry them at home.

Triple Chocolate PB Minis

2 packages (4.4 ounces each) chocolate peanut butter cups*
1 package (about 18 ounces) chocolate fudge cake mix, plus ingredients
    to prepare mix
¾ cup whipping cream
1½ cups semisweet chocolate chips

*Freeze candy to make chopping easier.

1. Preheat oven to 350°F. Line 60 mini (1¾-inch) muffin cups with paper baking cups. Finely chop peanut butter cups; refrigerate while preparing batter.

2. Prepare cake mix according to package directions; stir in 1 cup chopped peanut butter cups. Spoon batter into prepared muffin cups, filling two-thirds full.

3. Bake 10 minutes or until toothpick inserted into centers comes out clean. Cool in pans 5 minutes. Remove to wire racks; cool completely.

4. Meanwhile, bring cream to a simmer in small saucepan over medium heat. Place chocolate chips in small bowl; pour cream over top. Let stand 5 minutes; whisk until chocolate is melted and mixture is smooth. Glaze will thicken as it cools (or refrigerate glaze to thicken more quickly).

5. Dip tops of cupcakes in glaze; sprinkle with remaining chopped candy. Place on wire racks; let stand until glaze is set. *Makes 60 mini cupcakes*

Lemon Meringue Cupcakes

1 package (about 18 ounces) lemon cake mix, plus ingredients
    to prepare mix
¾ cup prepared lemon curd*
4 egg whites, at room temperature
6 tablespoons sugar

Lemon curd, a thick sweet lemon spread, is available in many supermarkets near the jams and preserves.

1. Preheat oven to 350°F. Line 9 jumbo (3½-inch) muffin cups with paper baking cups. Prepare cake mix according to package directions. Spoon batter into prepared muffin cups, filling two-thirds full.

2. Bake 20 to 25 minutes or until toothpick inserted into centers comes out clean. Cool in pans 10 minutes. Remove to wire racks; cool completely. *Increase oven temperature to 375°F.*

3. Cut off tops of cupcakes with serrated knife. (Do not remove paper baking cups.) Scoop out small hole in center of each cupcake with tablespoon; fill with generous tablespoon lemon curd. Replace cupcake tops.

4. Beat egg whites in medium bowl with electric mixer at high speed until soft peaks form. Gradually add sugar, beating until stiff peaks form. Pipe or spread meringue in peaks on each cupcake.

5. Place cupcakes on baking sheet. Bake 5 minutes or until peaks of meringue are golden. *Makes 9 jumbo cupcakes*

Variation: This recipe can also be used to make 24 standard (2½-inch) cupcakes. Line muffin pans with paper baking cups. Prepare and bake cake mix according to package directions. Cut off tops of cupcakes; scoop out hole in each cupcake with teaspoon and fill with generous teaspoon lemon curd. Pipe or spread meringue in peaks on each cupcake; bake as directed above.

 Divine Desserts

German Chocolate Cupcakes

1 package (about 18 ounces) German chocolate cake mix, plus ingredients
   to prepare mix
1 can (12 ounces) evaporated milk
¾ cup granulated sugar
½ cup (1 stick) butter, softened
4 egg yolks, beaten
¼ cup brown sugar
2 cups shredded coconut
1 cup chopped pecans
3 ounces semisweet chocolate, finely chopped

1. Preheat oven to 350°F. Line 22 standard (2½-inch) muffin cups with paper baking cups.

2. Prepare cake mix according to package directions. Spoon batter into prepared muffin cups, filling two-thirds full. Bake 20 minutes or until toothpick inserted into centers comes out clean. Cool in pans 10 minutes. Remove to wire racks; cool completely.

3. Combine evaporated milk, granulated sugar, butter, egg yolks and brown sugar in medium saucepan. Cook over medium-low heat 8 to 10 minutes or until slightly thickened and just beginning to bubble, stirring constantly. Stir in coconut and pecans. Remove from heat; let stand 1 hour or until thickened, stirring occasionally. Spoon cooled coconut mixture evenly over each cupcake.

4. Place chocolate in small microwavable bowl; microwave on HIGH 30 seconds; stir. Microwave at additional 15-second intervals until chocolate is melted. Drizzle over cupcakes. *Makes 22 cupcakes*

 *Divine Desserts*

Key Lime Pie Cupcakes

   1 package (about 18 ounces) lemon cake mix with pudding in the mix
   1 cup vegetable oil
   4 eggs
   ¾ cup key lime juice,* divided
   ½ cup water
   1 teaspoon grated lime peel
   2 cups whipping cream
   ½ cup powdered sugar
       Lime wedges or additional grated lime peel (optional)

If you cannot find key lime juice, substitute regular lime juice.

1. Preheat oven to 350°F. Line 24 standard (2½-inch) muffin cups with paper baking cups.

2. Combine cake mix, oil, eggs, ½ cup key lime juice, water and lime peel in large bowl; whisk 2 minutes or until thick and smooth. Spoon batter into prepared muffin cups, filling two-thirds full. Bake 20 minutes or until toothpick inserted into centers comes out clean. Cool in pans 10 minutes. Remove to wire racks; cool completely.

3. Beat cream in medium bowl with electric mixer at medium speed 3 to 5 minutes or until soft peaks form. Add powdered sugar and remaining ¼ cup key lime juice; beat at medium-high speed 30 seconds or until medium-stiff peaks form.

4. Top each cupcake with whipped cream. Garnish with lime wedges. Serve immediately.
Makes 24 cupcakes

 Divine Desserts

Peppermint Mocha Cupcakes

1 package (about 18 ounces) dark chocolate cake mix, plus ingredients
    to prepare mix
1 tablespoon instant espresso powder
1½ cups whipping cream
1 package (12 ounces) semisweet chocolate chips
2 teaspoons peppermint extract
  Crushed candy canes or peppermint candies

1. Preheat oven to 350°F. Line 24 standard (2½-inch) muffin cups with paper baking cups. Prepare cake mix according to package directions; stir in espresso powder. Spoon batter evenly into prepared muffin cups.

2. Bake 20 minutes or until toothpick inserted into centers comes out clean. Cool in pans 10 minutes. Remove to wire racks; cool completely.

3. Bring cream to a simmer in small saucepan over medium heat. Place chocolate chips in medium bowl; pour cream over top. Let stand 2 minutes; whisk until chocolate is melted and mixture is smooth. Stir in peppermint extract.

4. Place wire rack over waxed paper. Dip tops of cupcakes in chocolate mixture; place on rack. Let stand 10 minutes; repeat, if desired. Sprinkle tops with crushed candy canes. *Makes 24 cupcakes*

TIP

The amount of instant espresso powder in this recipe will not produce cupcakes with a distinct coffee flavor. It merely adds to the richness and complexity of the chocolate flavor of the cupcakes.

 *Divine Desserts*

Carrot Cream Cheese Cupcakes

1 package (8 ounces) cream cheese, softened
¼ cup powdered sugar
1 package (about 18 ounces) spice cake mix, plus ingredients
    to prepare mix
2 cups grated carrots
2 tablespoons finely chopped crystallized ginger
1 container (16 ounces) cream cheese frosting
3 tablespoons maple syrup
  Orange peel strips (optional)

1. Preheat oven to 350°F. Spray 14 jumbo (3½-inch) muffin cups with nonstick cooking spray or line with paper baking cups.

2. Beat cream cheese and powdered sugar in large bowl with electric mixer at medium speed 1 minute or until light and fluffy. Cover and refrigerate.

3. Prepare cake mix according to package directions; stir in carrots and ginger. Spoon batter into prepared muffin cups, filling one-third full. Place 1 tablespoon cream cheese mixture in center of each cup. Top evenly with remaining batter.

4. Bake 25 to 28 minutes or until toothpick inserted into centers comes out clean. Cool in pans 10 minutes. Remove to wire racks; cool completely.

5. Combine frosting and maple syrup in medium bowl until well blended. Frost cupcakes; garnish with orange peel. *Makes 14 jumbo cupcakes*

 Divine Desserts

Whoopie Pie Cupcakes

1 package (about 18 ounces) dark chocolate cake mix, plus ingredients
    to prepare mix
½ cup (1 stick) unsalted butter, softened
¼ cup shortening
3 cups powdered sugar
⅓ cup whipping cream
1 teaspoon salt

1. Preheat oven to 350°F. Grease 24 standard (2½-inch) muffin cups. Prepare cake mix according to package directions. Spoon batter into prepared muffin cups, filling two-thirds full.

2. Bake 20 minutes or until toothpick inserted into centers comes out clean. Cool in pans 10 minutes. Remove to wire racks; cool completely.

3. Beat butter and shortening in large bowl with electric mixer at medium speed until well blended. Add powdered sugar, cream and salt; beat at low speed 1 minute. Beat at medium-high speed 2 minutes or until fluffy.

4. Slice tops off cupcakes. Spread filling over bottoms of cupcakes; replace tops.

Makes 24 cupcakes

 *Divine Desserts*

Limoncello Cupcakes

Cupcakes
- 1 package (about 18 ounces) lemon cake mix
- 4 eggs
- 1 package (4-serving size) lemon instant pudding and pie filling mix
- ½ cup vegetable oil
- ½ cup vodka
- ½ cup water

Glaze
- 4 cups powdered sugar
- ⅓ cup lemon juice
- 3 to 4 tablespoons vodka
- Candied lemon peel
- Coarse sugar (optional)

1. Preheat oven to 350°F. Line 24 standard (2½-inch) muffin cups with paper baking cups.

2. Beat cake mix, eggs, pudding mix, oil, ½ cup vodka and water in large bowl with electric mixer at low speed until smooth. Spoon batter evenly into prepared muffin cups. Bake 15 minutes or until toothpick inserted into centers comes out clean. Cool completely in pans on wire racks.

3. For glaze, whisk powdered sugar, lemon juice and 3 tablespoons vodka in medium bowl until smooth. Add remaining 1 tablespoon vodka if icing is too stiff. Dip tops of cupcakes in glaze; garnish with candied lemon peel. Sprinkle with coarse sugar, if desired. Let stand until set. *Makes 24 cupcakes*

 *Divine Desserts*

Rocky Road Cupcakes

1 package (about 18 ounces) chocolate fudge cake mix
1⅓ cups water
3 eggs
½ cup vegetable oil
¾ cup mini semisweet chocolate chips, divided
1 container (16 ounces) chocolate frosting
1 cup mini marshmallows
⅔ cup walnut pieces
   Hot fudge ice cream topping or chocolate syrup, heated

1. Preheat oven to 325°F. Line 22 standard (2½-inch) muffin cups with paper baking cups.

2. Beat cake mix, water, eggs, oil and ¼ cup chocolate chips in large bowl with electric mixer at low speed 30 seconds. Beat at medium speed 2 minutes or until well blended. Spoon batter into prepared muffin cups, filling two-thirds full.

3. Bake 20 minutes or until toothpick inserted into centers comes out clean. Cool in pans 10 minutes. Remove to wire racks; cool completely.

4. Spread thin layer of frosting over cupcakes. Top with marshmallows, walnuts and remaining ½ cup chocolate chips, pressing down lightly to adhere to frosting. Drizzle with hot fudge topping.   *Makes 22 cupcakes*

 *Divine Desserts*

Banana Cream Pie Cupcakes

1 package (about 18 ounces) yellow cake mix, plus ingredients to
    prepare mix
1 package (4-serving size) banana instant pudding and pie filling mix
2 cups cold milk
2 bananas
2 tablespoons sugar, divided
2 cups cold whipping cream

1. Preheat oven to 350°F. Line 24 standard (2½-inch) muffin cups with paper baking cups. Prepare cake mix according to package directions. Spoon batter evenly into prepared muffin cups.

2. Bake 20 minutes or until toothpick inserted into centers comes out clean. Cool in pans 10 minutes. Remove to wire racks; cool completely.

3. Prepare pudding using milk according to package directions. Cover and refrigerate until set.

4. Preheat broiler. Line baking sheet with parchment paper. Cut each banana into 12 slices. Place 1 tablespoon sugar in shallow bowl. Dip one side of banana slices into sugar; place sugar side up on prepared baking sheet. Broil 2 minutes or until golden brown; remove from broiler immediately. Cool completely.

5. Beat cream and remaining 1 tablespoon sugar in large bowl with electric mixer at medium-high speed until stiff peaks form.

6. Cut 1-inch hole in top of each cupcake with paring knife. Fill with pudding; reserve remaining pudding for another use. Place whipped cream in pastry bag fitted with large star tip; pipe onto cupcakes. Top each cupcake with banana slice. *Makes 24 cupcakes*

 *Divine Desserts*

Mini Tiramisu Cupcakes

2 teaspoons instant espresso powder
1 tablespoon hot water
1 tablespoon coffee liqueur
1 package (about 18 ounces) butter recipe yellow cake mix
3 eggs
⅔ cup water
½ cup (1 stick) butter, softened and cut into small pieces
1 package (8 ounces) mascarpone cheese*
½ cup powdered sugar
¼ teaspoon vanilla
½ (8-ounce) container French vanilla whipped topping
   Unsweetened cocoa powder

Mascarpone cheese is an Italian soft cheese that is a traditional ingredient in tiramisu. Look for it in the specialty cheese section of the supermarket.

1. Preheat oven to 350°F. Line 18 standard (2½-inch) muffin cups with paper baking cups. Stir espresso powder into hot water in medium bowl until dissolved. Add liqueur; mix well.

2. Beat cake mix, eggs, water and butter in large bowl with electric mixer at medium speed 3 minutes or until smooth. Transfer half of batter to coffee mixture; mix well. Spoon equal amounts of coffee and plain batters into each prepared muffin cup, filling three-fourths full. Swirl batters with toothpick or paring knife.

3. Bake 16 to 18 minutes or until toothpick inserted into centers comes out clean. Cool in pans 10 minutes. Remove to wire racks; cool completely.

4. For filling, combine mascarpone cheese, powdered sugar and vanilla in medium bowl. Fold in whipped topping.

5. Cut off tops of cupcakes; cut out designs in center of cupcake tops with mini cookie cutters.

6. Spoon filling evenly over cupcake bottoms. Sprinkle cupcake tops with cocoa; place over filling. Refrigerate 2 hours before serving.   *Makes 18 cupcakes*

 *Divine Desserts*

Pineapple Upside-Down Cupcakes

1 cup packed brown sugar
1 can (20 ounces) pineapple chunks in syrup, drained and ¼ cup
    syrup reserved
1 package (about 18 ounces) yellow cake mix, plus ingredients
    to prepare mix
12 maraschino cherries, halved

1. Preheat oven to 350°F. Spray 24 standard (2½-inch) muffin cups with nonstick cooking spray.

2. Place 2 teaspoons brown sugar in each prepared muffin cup. Cut 2 pineapple chunks horizontally to create 4 wedge-shaped pieces. Arrange pineapple pieces over brown sugar for flower petals.

3. Prepare cake mix according to package directions, substituting ¼ cup of pineapple syrup for ¼ cup of water indicated. Spoon batter over pineapple in muffin cups, filling three-fourths full.

4. Bake 20 minutes or until toothpick inserted into centers comes out clean. Cool in pans 10 minutes. Remove from pans. Place cupcakes on serving plate, pineapple side up. Place cherry half on center of each cupcake.

Makes 24 cupcakes

Prep Time: 25 minutes
Bake Time: 20 minutes

 *Divine Desserts*

Chocolate Chip Cookie Cupcakes

1 package (about 18 ounces) yellow cake mix, plus ingredients
    to prepare mix
1½ cups semisweet chocolate chips, divided
1½ cups chopped walnuts or pecans, divided
1 container (16 ounces) cream cheese frosting
¾ cup creamy peanut butter

1. Preheat oven to 350°F. Line 24 standard (2½-inch) muffin cups with paper baking cups.

2. Prepare cake mix according to package directions. Stir in ¾ cup chocolate chips and ¾ cup walnuts. Spoon batter into prepared muffin cups, filling two-thirds full.

3. Bake 20 minutes or until toothpick inserted into centers comes out clean. Cool in pans 10 minutes. Remove to wire racks; cool completely.

4. Combine frosting and peanut butter in medium bowl until well blended. Frost cupcakes; sprinkle with remaining ¾ cup chocolate chips and ¾ cup walnuts.

Makes 24 cupcakes

TIP

These delightful cupcakes combine all the classic flavors of nutty chocolate chip cookies, making them perfect for a very special after-school treat. Feel free to omit the nuts if allergies are a concern.

Sweet Little Sheep

- 1 package (about 18 ounces) cake mix, any flavor, plus ingredients to prepare mix
- 1 container (16 ounces) white frosting
- 2 packages (10½ ounces each) mini marshmallows
  Chewy chocolate candies
  Small white and pink round decors
  Black decorating gel

1. Preheat oven to 350°F. Line 60 mini (1¾-inch) muffin cups with paper baking cups. Prepare cake mix according to package directions. Spoon batter into prepared muffin cups, filling almost full.

2. Bake 10 minutes or until toothpick inserted into centers comes out clean. Cool in pans 10 minutes. Remove to wire racks; cool completely.

3. Frost cupcakes. Press marshmallows into frosting, completely covering cupcakes.

4. Unwrap chewy chocolate candies; cut off small piece of each candy to use for ears and reserve. Working with one large piece at a time, microwave on LOW (30%) 5 seconds or until slightly softened. For heads, press candy between hands or on waxed paper to flatten slightly; form into oblong shape. For ears, cut reserved small pieces of candy in half. Shape each half into triangle.

5. Place candy head on one side of each cupcake. Attach decors for noses and ears to head using small dabs of frosting. Add dot of decorating gel to each eye.

Makes 60 sheep

Pink Piglets

1 package (about 18 ounces) yellow cake mix, plus ingredients
    to prepare mix
1 container (16 ounces) white frosting
  Pink or red food coloring
  Mini semisweet chocolate chips
  Small fruit-flavored pastel candy wafers
  Red or pink chewy fruit candy squares

1. Preheat oven to 350°F. Line 60 mini (1¾-inch) muffin cups with paper baking cups. Prepare cake mix according to package directions. Spoon batter evenly into prepared muffin cups, filling almost full.

2. Bake 15 minutes or until toothpick inserted into centers comes out clean. Cool in pans 10 minutes. Remove to wire racks; cool completely.

3. Place frosting in medium bowl; add food coloring, a few drops at a time, until desired shade of pink is reached. Frost cupcakes. Create faces at one end of each cupcake using chocolate chips for eyes and candy wafers for noses.

4. Working with one at a time, unwrap candy squares and microwave on LOW (30%) 5 to 10 seconds or until softened. Press candies between hands or on waxed paper to flatten to ⅛-inch thickness. Use scissors or paring knife to cut out triangles for ears; fold over top corner of each triangle. Arrange ears on cupcakes.

5. Cut ⅛-inch strips, 1 to 2 inches long, from flattened candies. Shape candy strips into spirals for tails; place candies in freezer 10 minutes to set. Place tails on cupcakes. *Makes 60 piglets*

 *On the Wild Side*

Monkey A-Rounds

1 package (about 18 ounces) chocolate cake mix, plus ingredients
    to prepare mix
1 container (16 ounces) chocolate frosting
1 container (16 ounces) white frosting
    Yellow food coloring
44 chocolate discs
    Small black jelly beans
    Black string licorice

1. Preheat oven to 350°F. Line 22 standard (2½-inch) muffin cups with paper baking cups. Prepare cake mix according to package directions. Spoon batter into prepared muffin cups, filling two-thirds full.

2. Bake 20 minutes or until toothpick inserted into centers comes out clean. Cool in pans 10 minutes. Remove to wire racks; cool completely.

3. Frost cupcakes with chocolate frosting. Place white frosting in small bowl. Add food coloring, a few drops at a time, until desired shade of yellow is reached. Transfer frosting to pastry bag or small food storage bag with small corner cut off.

4. Pipe circle of yellow frosting in center of each chocolate disc for ears. Cut jelly beans in half crosswise for eyes; cut licorice into shorter lengths for mouths and noses. Pipe yellow frosting into oval shape on each cupcake as shown in photo; arrange eyes just above oval and ears on either side of cupcake. Arrange licorice noses and mouths inside oval. Use toothpick or knife to pull up frosting at top of cupcake for hair. *Makes 22 cupcakes*

 On the Wild Side

Mini Mice

1 package (about 18 ounces) chocolate cake mix, plus ingredients
    to prepare mix
1 container (16 ounces) chocolate frosting
1 container (16 ounces) white frosting (optional)
    Small black and pink hard candies or decors
    Small fruit-flavored pastel candy wafers
    Black string licorice

1. Preheat oven to 350°F. Line 60 mini (1¾-inch) muffin cups with paper baking cups. Prepare cake mix according to package directions. Spoon batter into prepared muffin cups, filling almost full.

2. Bake 12 minutes or until toothpick inserted into centers comes out clean. Cool in pans 10 minutes. Remove to wire racks; cool completely.

3. For brown mice, frost cupcakes with chocolate frosting; use knife or small spatula to pull up frosting and create fuzzy appearance. For speckled mice, frost cupcakes with white frosting; use toothpick to add streaks of chocolate frosting.

4. Arrange candies on one side of each cupcake for eyes, nose and ears. Cut licorice into 3-inch lengths; press into opposite end of each cupcake for tail.

Makes 60 mice

Mini Bees

1 package (about 18 ounces) chocolate cake mix, plus ingredients
    to prepare mix
1 container (16 ounces) chocolate frosting
1½ cups prepared white frosting
    Yellow food coloring
    Black string licorice
    Yellow candy wafers

1. Preheat oven to 350°F. Line 60 mini (1¾-inch) muffin cups with paper baking cups. Prepare cake mix according to package directions. Spoon batter into prepared muffin cups, filling half full.

2. Bake 10 minutes or until toothpick inserted into centers comes out clean. Cool in pans 5 minutes. Remove to wire racks; cool completely.

3. Microwave chocolate frosting in medium microwavable bowl on LOW (30%) 30 seconds; stir until melted. Dip tops of cupcakes in melted frosting; place on baking sheet. (Frosting may need to be reheated several times to maintain melted consistency.) Refrigerate cupcakes 10 minutes or until frosting is set before adding stripes. Reserve remaining chocolate frosting.

4. Place white frosting in medium bowl; add food coloring, a few drops at a time, until desired shade of yellow is reached. Spoon frosting into pastry bag fitted with small round tip or resealable food storage bag with ⅛-inch corner cut off. Pipe stripes on cupcakes.

5. Pipe reserved chocolate frosting for eyes and mouths, reheating, if necessary, to achieve smooth consistency. Cut licorice into 1½-inch lengths; place on cupcakes just above eyes for antennae and at opposite end for stingers. Cut candy wafers in half; arrange two halves on each cupcake for wings.

Makes 60 bees

 On the Wild Side

Hedgehogs

1 package (about 18 ounces) chocolate cake mix, plus ingredients
    to prepare mix
1 container (16 ounces) chocolate frosting
  Black jelly beans
  Small round white candies
  Black decorating gel
  Candy-coated licorice pieces

1. Preheat oven to 350°F. Place 22 standard (2-inch) silicone muffin cups on large baking sheet or line 22 standard (2½-inch) muffin cups with paper baking cups.

2. Prepare cake mix according to package directions. Spoon batter into prepared muffin cups, filling two-thirds full.

3. Bake 20 minutes or until toothpick inserted into centers comes out clean. If using pans, cool in pans 10 minutes. Remove to wire racks; cool completely.

4. Frost cupcakes. Cut jelly beans in half crosswise for noses. Arrange jelly bean halves and round candies on one side of each cupcake for faces; pipe dot of decorating gel onto each eye. Arrange licorice pieces around face and all over each cupcake. *Makes 22 cupcakes*

Black Cat Cupcakes

1 package (about 18 ounces) cake mix, any flavor, plus ingredients
　　to prepare mix
1 container (16 ounces) chocolate fudge frosting
　White decorating icing
　Graham crackers
　Black string licorice
　Assorted candies

1. Preheat oven to 350°F. Line 24 standard (2½-inch) muffin cups with paper baking cups.

2. Prepare cake mix according to package directions. Spoon batter into prepared muffin cups, filling two-thirds full.

3. Bake 20 minutes or until toothpick inserted into centers comes out clean. Cool in pans 10 minutes. Remove to wire racks; cool completely.

4. Frost cupcakes. Pipe two mounds in center of each cupcake for cheeks. Pipe mouths using white decorating icing. Cut graham crackers into small triangles; press into cupcakes for ears. Decorate cat faces with licorice and assorted candies. *Makes 24 cupcakes*

 On the Wild Side

Fishy Friends

1 package (about 18 ounces) cake mix, any flavor, plus ingredients
    to prepare mix
1 container (16 ounces) white frosting
    Orange, purple and blue food coloring
    Assorted colored jelly candy fruit slices
    White round candies
    Colored round gummy candies
    Black decorating gel

1. Preheat oven to 350°F. Line 22 standard (2½-inch) muffin cups with paper baking cups. Prepare cake mix according to package directions. Spoon batter into prepared muffin cups, filling two-thirds full.

2. Bake 20 minutes or until toothpick inserted into centers comes out clean. Cool in pans 10 minutes. Remove to wire racks; cool completely.

3. Divide frosting among three small bowls. Add food coloring, a few drops at a time, until desired shades are reached. Frost cupcakes.

4. Cut jelly candies into triangles for fins and tails. Arrange white candies and gummy candies at one end of each cupcake for faces; add dot of decorating gel to each eye. Arrange jelly candy triangles on top and side of each cupcake.

Makes 22 cupcakes

 On the Wild Side

Leopard Spots

1 package (about 18 ounces) dark chocolate cake mix, plus ingredients
    to prepare mix
3 cups powdered sugar, sifted
½ cup (1 stick) unsalted butter, softened
3 to 4 tablespoons milk, divided
½ teaspoon vanilla
    Brown and yellow gel food coloring
    Black and orange decorating gels

1. Preheat oven to 350°F. Line 24 standard (2½-inch) muffin cups with paper baking cups. Prepare cake mix according to package directions. Spoon batter into prepared muffin cups, filling two-thirds full.

2. Bake 20 minutes or until toothpick inserted into centers comes out clean. Cool in pans 10 minutes. Remove to wire racks; cool completely.

3. Beat powdered sugar, butter, 2 tablespoons milk and vanilla in large bowl with electric mixer at low speed until blended. Beat at high speed until light and fluffy, adding additional milk, 1 teaspoon at a time, to reach spreading consistency. Tint frosting with food coloring to make sandy color.

4. Pipe spots all over tops of cupcakes using black gel for outline and orange gel for centers.

Makes 24 cupcakes

 *On the Wild Side*

Chocolate Moose

1 package (about 18 ounces) chocolate cake mix, plus ingredients
   to prepare mix
1 container (16 ounces) milk chocolate frosting
½ to ¾ cup vanilla frosting
1 package (12 ounces) semisweet chocolate chips
2 tablespoons shortening
   White round candies
   Small black candies
   Black decorating gel
   Pretzel twists

1. Preheat oven to 350°F. Line 22 standard (2½-inch) muffin cups with paper baking cups. Prepare cake mix according to package directions. Spoon batter into prepared muffin cups, filling two-thirds full.

2. Bake 20 minutes or until toothpick inserted into centers comes out clean. Cool in pans 10 minutes. Remove to wire racks; cool completely.

3. Combine chocolate frosting and ½ cup vanilla frosting in medium bowl until well blended. (Stir in additional vanilla frosting if lighter color is desired.) Frost cupcakes.

4. Place chocolate chips and shortening in medium microwavable bowl. Microwave on HIGH 1½ minutes or until chocolate is melted and mixture is smooth, stirring every 30 seconds. Place chocolate in pastry bag fitted with small round tip or medium food storage bag with small corner cut off. Pipe chocolate mixture into shape of moose head on each cupcake as shown in photo; smooth chocolate with small spatula. (Chocolate may need to be reheated slightly if it becomes too stiff to pipe.)

5. Arrange candies on cupcakes for eyes and noses. Pipe small dot of decorating gel onto each white candy for eyes. Break off small section of each pretzel twist to form antlers. Push ends of pretzels into tops of cupcakes.

Makes 22 cupcakes

 On the Wild Side

Friendly Frogs

1 package (about 18 ounces) cake mix, any flavor, plus ingredients
    to prepare mix
1 container (16 ounces) white frosting
  Green food coloring
  Green decorating sugar (optional)
  Black round candies or candy-coated chocolate pieces
  White chocolate candy discs
  Black and red string licorice
  Green jelly candy fruit slices (optional)

1. Preheat oven to 350°F. Line 22 standard (2½-inch) muffin cups with paper baking cups. Prepare cake mix according to package directions. Spoon batter into prepared muffin cups, filling two-thirds full.

2. Bake 20 minutes or until toothpick inserted into centers comes out clean. Cool in pans 10 minutes. Remove to wire racks; cool completely.

3. Place frosting in small bowl. Add food coloring, a few drops at a time, until desired shade of green is reached. Frost cupcakes; sprinkle with decorating sugar, if desired.

4. Use small dab of frosting to attach black candies to white discs for eyes. Cut licorice into shorter lengths for mouths and noses. Arrange candies on cupcakes for frog faces.

5. Use scissors to cut jelly candies into feet, if desired. Place cupcakes on candy feet just before serving.

Makes 22 cupcakes

 On the Wild Side

Zebra Stripes

1 package (about 18 ounces) dark chocolate cake mix, plus ingredients
    to prepare mix
24 ounces white chocolate
8 ounces whipping cream
    Black decorating icing

1. Preheat oven to 350°F. Line 24 standard (2½-inch) muffin cups with paper baking cups. Prepare cake mix according to package directions. Spoon batter evenly into prepared muffin cups.

2. Bake 20 minutes or until toothpick inserted into centers comes out clean. Cool in pans 10 minutes. Remove to wire racks; cool completely.

3. Chop white chocolate; place in medium bowl. Bring cream to a simmer in small saucepan over medium heat; pour over chocolate. Let stand 5 minutes; whisk until chocolate is melted and mixture is smooth. Let stand 5 minutes or until slightly thickened.

4. Place wire racks over waxed paper. Dip tops of cupcakes in glaze; place on racks. Let stand 10 minutes or until set.

5. Pipe stripes on tops of cupcakes with black decorating icing.

Makes 24 cupcakes

Fortune Teller Cupcakes

1 package (about 18 ounces) dark chocolate cake mix, plus ingredients
    to prepare mix
1½ cups whipping cream
1 package (12 ounces) semisweet chocolate chips
    Black gel food coloring
    Prepared white frosting
    Black decorating gel

1. Preheat oven to 350°F. Line 24 standard (2½-inch) muffin cups with paper baking cups. Prepare cake mix according to package directions. Spoon batter into prepared muffin cups, filling two-thirds full.

2. Bake 20 minutes or until toothpick inserted into centers comes out clean. Cool in pans 10 minutes. Remove to wire racks; cool completely.

3. Bring cream to a simmer in small saucepan over medium heat. Place chocolate chips in medium bowl; pour cream over top. Let stand 2 minutes; whisk until chocolate is melted and mixture is smooth. Add food coloring, a few drops at a time, to reach desired shade of black.

4. Place wire rack over waxed paper. Dip tops of cupcakes into chocolate mixture; place on wire rack. Allow to set; dip a second time, if desired. Pipe circles or triangle in center of each cupcake with frosting; smooth gently.

5. For numbered balls, pipe "8" in center of each white circle with decorating gel. For fortunes, pipe short messages like "yes" or "no" in center of each white triangle with decorating gel. *Makes 24 cupcakes*

 *Whimsy and Wit*

Dragonflies

1 package (about 18 ounces) cake mix, any flavor, plus ingredients
    to prepare mix
  White confectionery coating*
  Pink, purple, yellow and green food coloring
44 small pretzel twists
22 (2½-inch) pretzel sticks
  White and purple nonpareils
  Silver dragées
1 container (16 ounces) white frosting

Confectionery coating, also called almond bark or candy coating, can be found at craft stores and in the baking section of the supermarket. It comes in blocks, discs and chips and is usually available in white, milk and dark chocolate varieties.

1. Preheat oven to 350°F. Line 22 standard (2½-inch) muffin cups with paper baking cups. Prepare cake mix according to package directions. Spoon batter into prepared muffin cups, filling two-thirds full.

2. Bake 20 minutes or until toothpick inserted into centers comes out clean. Cool in pans 10 minutes. Remove to wire racks; cool completely.

3. Line large baking sheet with waxed paper. Melt confectionery coating according to package directions. Stir in pink food coloring, a few drops at a time, until desired shade of pink is reached. Dip pretzel twists in melted coating; arrange two twists together on prepared baking sheet. Dip pretzel sticks in coating; place one stick between two pretzel twists to create dragonfly. Sprinkle pretzel twists with white nonpareils; arrange two purple nonpareils at top of pretzel sticks for eyes. Press dragées into bottom half of pretzel sticks. Let stand 10 minutes or until set.

4. Meanwhile, divide frosting among three small bowls. Add different food coloring (except pink) to each bowl, a few drops at a time, until desired shades are reached. Pipe or spread frosting on cupcakes; top with dragonflies.

Makes 22 cupcakes

 Whimsy and Wit

Sunny Side Upcakes

1 package (about 18 ounces) vanilla cake mix, plus ingredients
    to prepare mix
22 yellow chewy fruit candy squares
2 containers (16 ounces each) white frosting

1. Preheat oven to 350°F. Line 22 standard (2½-inch) muffin cups with paper baking cups. Prepare cake mix according to package directions. Spoon batter into prepared muffin cups, filling two-thirds full.

2. Bake 20 minutes or until toothpick inserted into centers comes out clean. Cool in pans 10 minutes. Remove to wire racks; cool completely.

3. For each egg yolk, unwrap 1 candy square and microwave on LOW (30%) 5 seconds or just until softened. Shape into ball; flatten slightly.

4. Place 1 cup frosting in small microwavable bowl; microwave on LOW (30%) 10 seconds or until softened. Working with one cupcake at a time, spoon about 2 tablespoons frosting in center of cupcake. Spread frosting toward edges of cupcake in uneven petal shape to resemble egg white. Press candy into frosting in center of cupcake. Microwave additional frosting as needed.

Makes 22 cupcakes

Tropical Luau Cupcakes

2 cans (8 ounces each) crushed pineapple in juice
1 package (about 18 ounces) yellow cake mix *without* pudding
  in the mix
1 package (4-serving size) banana cream instant pudding and
  pie filling mix
4 eggs
⅓ cup vegetable oil
¼ teaspoon ground nutmeg
1 container (12 ounces) whipped vanilla frosting
¾ cup shredded coconut, toasted*
3 to 4 medium kiwi
30 (2½-inch) pretzel sticks

To toast coconut, spread evenly on ungreased baking sheet. Toast in preheated 350°F oven 5 to 7 minutes or until light golden brown, stirring occasionally.

1. Preheat oven to 350°F. Line 30 standard (2½-inch) muffin cups with paper baking cups. Drain pineapple, reserving juice.

2. Beat cake mix, pudding mix, eggs, oil, reserved pineapple juice and nutmeg in large bowl with electric mixer at low speed 1 minute or until blended. Beat at medium speed 2 minutes or until smooth. Fold in pineapple. Spoon batter into prepared muffin cups, filling two-thirds full.

3. Bake 20 minutes or until toothpick inserted into centers comes out clean. Cool in pans 10 minutes. Remove to wire racks; cool completely.

4. Frost cupcakes; sprinkle with coconut. For palm trees,** peel kiwi and cut into ⅛-inch-thick slices. Cut small notches around edges of kiwi slices for palm fronds. For palm tree trunk, push pretzel stick into, but not through, center of each kiwi slice. Push other end of pretzel into top of each cupcake.   *Makes 30 cupcakes*

**Palm tree decorations can be made up to 1 hour before serving.*

Snowy Peaks

1 package (about 18 ounces) chocolate cake mix, plus ingredients
    to prepare mix
4 egg whites, at room temperature
6 tablespoons sugar

1. Preheat oven to 350°F. Line 9 jumbo (3½-inch) muffin cups with paper baking cups. Prepare cake mix according to package directions. Spoon batter into prepared muffin cups, filling two-thirds full.

2. Bake 20 to 25 minutes or until toothpick inserted into centers comes out clean. Cool in pans 10 minutes. Remove to wire racks; cool completely.

3. *Increase oven temperature to 375°F.* Beat egg whites in medium bowl with electric mixer at high speed until soft peaks form. Gradually add sugar, beating until stiff peaks form. Pipe or spread meringue on each cupcake.

4. Place cupcakes on baking sheet. Bake 5 minutes or until peaks of meringue are golden.

Makes 9 jumbo cupcakes

TIP

The mixture of egg whites and sugar used to top these cupcakes is called meringue. Light and fluffy, it is different from the meringues you may be familiar with from the bakery or cookie aisle because it has not been baked at a low temperature to remove the moisture. Soft meringue, like this one, is often used as a topping for custard pies.

 *Whimsy and Wit*

Doodle Bug Cupcakes

1 package (about 18 ounces) white cake mix *without* pudding in the mix
1 cup sour cream
3 eggs
⅓ cup vegetable oil
⅓ cup water
1 teaspoon vanilla
1½ cups prepared cream cheese frosting
    Red, yellow, blue and green food coloring
    Red licorice strings, cut into 2-inch pieces
    Assorted round candies

1. Preheat oven to 350°F. Line 24 standard (2½-inch) muffin cups with paper baking cups.

2. Beat cake mix, sour cream, eggs, oil, water and vanilla in large bowl with electric mixer at low speed until blended. Beat at medium speed 2 minutes or until smooth. Spoon batter into prepared muffin cups, filling two-thirds full.

3. Bake 20 minutes or until toothpick inserted into centers comes out clean. Cool in pans 10 minutes. Remove to wire racks; cool completely.

4. Divide frosting evenly among four small bowls. Add different food coloring to each bowl, one drop at a time, until desired shades are reached. Frost cupcakes.

5. Make three small holes on opposite sides of each cupcake, making six holes total. Insert licorice pieces into holes for legs. Decorate tops of cupcakes with assorted candies.

Makes 24 cupcakes

 Whimsy and Wit

Under the Sea

1 package (about 18 ounces) cake mix, any flavor, plus ingredients
 to prepare mix
2 containers (16 ounces each) white frosting
 Blue, green, yellow, red and purple food coloring
 White decorating sugar (optional)
 Black decorating gel
 Assorted color decors, nonpareils and candy fish

1. Preheat oven to 350°F. Line 22 standard (2½-inch) muffin cups with paper baking cups. Prepare cake mix according to package directions. Spoon batter into prepared muffin cups, filling three-fourths full.

2. Bake 20 minutes or until toothpick inserted into centers comes out clean. Cool in pans 10 minutes. Remove to wire racks; cool completely.

3. Spoon one container of frosting into small bowl; add blue and green food coloring, a few drops at a time, until desired shade of aqua is reached. Spoon frosting into pastry bag fitted with large star tip. Pipe frosting in swirl pattern on cupcakes. Sprinkle with decorating sugar, if desired.

4. Divide remaining frosting among four bowls; add different food coloring (except blue) to each bowl, a few drops at a time, until desired shades are reached. Spoon each color into pastry bag fitted with small round tip or food storage bags with small corner cut off. Pipe sea creatures and plants on cupcakes: yellow fish, red crabs, purple starfish and green seaweed. Decorate with decorating gel, decors and candies.   *Makes 22 cupcakes*

 Whimsy and Wit

Fairy Tale Cupcakes

1 package (about 18 ounces) cake mix, any flavor, plus ingredients
    to prepare mix
1 container (16 ounces) white frosting
    Pink, purple, blue and yellow food coloring
    Silver dragées
    Assorted decors

1. Preheat oven to 350°F. Line 22 standard (2½-inch) muffin cups with paper baking cups or spray with nonstick cooking spray.

2. Prepare cake mix according to package directions. Spoon batter into prepared muffin cups, filling two-thirds full. Bake 20 minutes or until toothpick inserted into centers comes out clean. Cool in pans 10 minutes. Remove to wire racks; cool completely.

3. Divide frosting among four bowls; add different food coloring to each bowl, a few drops at a time, until desired shades are reached. Frost cupcakes with pink, purple and blue frosting; smooth tops with small spatula.

4. Spoon yellow frosting into pastry bag with round decorating tip or small food storage bag with small corner cut off. Pipe crowns and wands on cupcakes; decorate with dragées and decors. *Makes 22 cupcakes*

 Whimsy and Wit

Blue Goo Cupcakes

1 package (about 18 ounces) white cake mix, plus ingredients
     to prepare mix
  Blue food coloring
1 package (6 ounces) blue gelatin
1⅓ cups boiling water
  Blue decorating icing

1. Preheat oven to 350°F. Line 24 standard (2½-inch) muffin cups with paper baking cups. Prepare cake mix according to package directions, adding food coloring, a few drops at a time, until desired shade of blue is reached. Spoon batter into prepared muffin cups, filling two-thirds full.

2. Bake 20 minutes or until toothpick inserted into centers comes out clean. Cool in pans 10 minutes. Remove to wire racks; cool completely.

3. Meanwhile, combine gelatin and water in small bowl. Stir 3 minutes or until gelatin is completely dissolved. Freeze mixture 40 minutes or until partially set, stirring often.

4. Pipe ring of blue icing around edge of each cupcake. Spoon 1 rounded tablespoon gelatin mixture onto each cupcake. *Makes 24 cupcakes*

TIP

> For a firm texture, or in extreme heat, chill until serving time. For a runny "blob" consistency, serve at room temperature.

Colorful Caterpillar Cupcakes

1 package (about 18 ounces) vanilla cake mix
1¼ cups water
3 eggs
⅓ cup vegetable oil
    Assorted food coloring
1 container (16 ounces) white frosting
    Assorted candies, candy-coated chocolate pieces, red string
        licorice and lollipops
    Gummy worms

1. Preheat oven to 350°F. Line 20 standard (2½-inch) muffin cups with paper baking cups.*

2. Beat cake mix, water, eggs and oil in large bowl with electric mixer at low speed 30 seconds. Beat at medium speed 2 minutes or until well blended. Divide batter among five bowls; add different food coloring to each bowl, a few drops at a time, until desired shades are reached. Spoon batter into prepared muffin cups, filling three-fourths full.

3. Bake 20 minutes or until toothpick inserted into centers comes out clean. Cool in pans 10 minutes. Remove to wire racks; cool completely.

4. Set aside two cupcakes for caterpillar head. Frost remaining cupcakes. Place one cupcake on its side at edge of serving plate. Place second cupcake on its side in front of first cupcake; arrange remaining cupcakes, alternating colors, in row to create body of caterpillar.

5. Frost one reserved cupcake; decorate with assorted candies, chocolate pieces, licorice and lollipops for face. Place plain cupcake upright at front of cupcake row for head; top with face cupcake on its side. Cut gummy worms into small pieces; attach to caterpillar body with frosting for legs.

Makes 20 cupcakes

Use white paper baking cups to best show colors of caterpillar.

 *Whimsy and Wit*

Billiard Ball Cupcakes

1 package (about 18 ounces) cake mix, any flavor, plus ingredients
    to prepare mix
6 cups powdered sugar, divided
1 cup (2 sticks) unsalted butter, softened
6 to 8 tablespoons milk, divided
1 teaspoon vanilla
    Assorted gel food coloring
    White wafer candy discs
    Black decorating gel

1. Preheat oven to 350°F. Line 24 standard (2½-inch) muffin cups with paper baking cups. Prepare cake mix according to package directions. Spoon batter evenly into prepared muffin cups.

2. Bake 20 minutes or until toothpick inserted into centers comes out clean. Cool in pans 10 minutes. Remove to wire racks; cool completely.

3. Combine 3 cups powdered sugar, butter, 4 tablespoons milk and vanilla in large bowl. Beat with electric mixer at low speed until smooth. Add remaining 3 cups powdered sugar; beat until light and fluffy, adding remaining milk, 1 tablespoon at a time, as needed for spreadable consistency.

4. Reserve one fourth of frosting. Divide remaining frosting evenly among small bowls; add different food coloring to each bowl, a few drops at a time, until desired shades are reached. For "solids," frost cupcakes with colored frosting. Place one candy disc in center of each cupcake.

5. For "stripes," frost cupcakes with reserved white frosting. Spread center two thirds of each cupcake with colored frosting. Place one candy disc in center of each cupcake.

6. Pipe number in center of each candy disc using decorating gel.

Makes 24 cupcakes

 *Whimsy and Wit*

Sweet Snowflakes

1 package (about 18 ounces) white cake mix, plus ingredients
    to prepare mix
4 ounces white chocolate candy discs or almond bark
    Silver, pearl or blue decorating sugar and decors
    White frosting

1. Preheat oven to 350°F. Line 24 standard (2½-inch) muffin cups with paper baking cups. Prepare cake mix according to package directions. Spoon batter into prepared muffin cups, filling two-thirds full.

2. Bake 20 minutes or until toothpick inserted into centers comes out clean. Cool in pans 10 minutes. Remove to wire racks; cool completely.

3. Place waxed paper on work surface. Melt candy discs according to package directions; place in plastic squeeze bottle or pastry bag fitted with small round tip. Pipe snowflake shapes onto waxed paper, a few at a time. Decorate with sugar and decors as desired. Repeat to create 24 large or 48 small snowflakes. Let stand 15 minutes.

4. Frost cupcakes; insert snowflakes into frosting.   *Makes 24 cupcakes*

 Whimsy and Wit

Colossal Birthday Cupcake

1 package (about 18 ounces) devil's food cake mix, plus ingredients
    to prepare mix
1 container (16 ounces) vanilla or chocolate frosting, divided
¼ cup peanut butter
    Construction paper or aluminum foil
    Fruit-flavored candy wafers or chocolate shavings

1. Preheat oven to 350°F. Grease and flour two 8-inch round cake pans.

2. Prepare cake mix according to package directions; pour batter evenly into prepared pans. Bake 30 minutes or until toothpick inserted into centers comes out clean. Cool completely in pans on wire racks.

3. Beat ¾ cup frosting and peanut butter in medium bowl. Place one cake layer on serving plate; spread evenly with peanut butter frosting. Top with remaining cake layer; spread top with remaining vanilla frosting, mounding frosting slightly higher in center.

4. Cut 36×3½-inch piece of construction paper; pleat paper every ½ inch. Wrap around side of cake to resemble baking cup. Decorate with candy wafers.

Makes 12 servings

Index

Index

Index

METRIC CONVERSION CHART

VOLUME MEASUREMENTS (dry)

1/8 teaspoon = 0.5 mL
1/4 teaspoon = 1 mL
1/2 teaspoon = 2 mL
3/4 teaspoon = 4 mL
1 teaspoon = 5 mL
1 tablespoon = 15 mL
2 tablespoons = 30 mL
1/4 cup = 60 mL
1/3 cup = 75 mL
1/2 cup = 125 mL
2/3 cup = 150 mL
3/4 cup = 175 mL
1 cup = 250 mL
2 cups = 1 pint = 500 mL
3 cups = 750 mL
4 cups = 1 quart = 1 L

VOLUME MEASUREMENTS (fluid)

1 fluid ounce (2 tablespoons) = 30 mL
4 fluid ounces (1/2 cup) = 125 mL
8 fluid ounces (1 cup) = 250 mL
12 fluid ounces (1 1/2 cups) = 375 mL
16 fluid ounces (2 cups) = 500 mL

WEIGHTS (mass)

1/2 ounce = 15 g
1 ounce = 30 g
3 ounces = 90 g
4 ounces = 120 g
8 ounces = 225 g
10 ounces = 285 g
12 ounces = 360 g
16 ounces = 1 pound = 450 g

DIMENSIONS

1/16 inch = 2 mm
1/8 inch = 3 mm
1/4 inch = 6 mm
1/2 inch = 1.5 cm
3/4 inch = 2 cm
1 inch = 2.5 cm

OVEN TEMPERATURES

250°F = 120°C
275°F = 140°C
300°F = 150°C
325°F = 160°C
350°F = 180°C
375°F = 190°C
400°F = 200°C
425°F = 220°C
450°F = 230°C

BAKING PAN SIZES

Utensil	Size in Inches/Quarts	Metric Volume	Size in Centimeters
Baking or Cake Pan (square or rectangular)	8×8×2	2 L	20×20×5
	9×9×2	2.5 L	23×23×5
	12×8×2	3 L	30×20×5
	13×9×2	3.5 L	33×23×5
Loaf Pan	8×4×3	1.5 L	20×10×7
	9×5×3	2 L	23×13×7
Round Layer Cake Pan	8×1½	1.2 L	20×4
	9×1½	1.5 L	23×4
Pie Plate	8×1¼	750 mL	20×3
	9×1¼	1 L	23×3
Baking Dish or Casserole	1 quart	1 L	—
	1½ quart	1.5 L	—
	2 quart	2 L	—